INNOCENT WITNESSES

# INNOCENT

*Childhood Memories of World War II*

# WITNESSES

MARILYN YALOM

*With a Foreword by* Meg Waite Clayton
*Edited by* Ben Yalom

REDWOOD PRESS
*Stanford, California*

STANFORD UNIVERSITY PRESS
Stanford, California

Printed in the United States of America on acid-free, archival-quality paper

Library of Congress Cataloging-in-Publication Data
Names: Yalom, Marilyn, author. | Clayton, Meg Waite, writer of foreword. | Yalom, Ben, editor.
Title: Innocent witnesses: childhood memories of World War II / Marilyn Yalom; with a foreword by Meg Waite Clayton; edited by Ben Yalom.
Description: Stanford, California : Redwood Press, [2021]
Identifiers: LCCN 2020026964 (print) | LCCN 2020026965 (ebook) | ISBN 9781503613652 (cloth) | ISBN 9781503614048 (epub)
Subjects: LCSH: World War, 1939-1945—Children—Europe. | World War, 1939-1945—Europe—Personal narratives. | LCGFT: Personal narratives.
Classification: LCC D810.C4 Y35 2021 (print) | LCC D810.C4 (ebook) | DDC 940.53092/53094—dc23
LC record available at https://lccn.loc.gov/2020026964
LC ebook record available at https://lccn.loc.gov/2020026965

Cover design: Rob Ehle

Cover photo: "Traces of the war, Freiburg after 1945." akg-images, Ltd.

Text design: Kevin Barrett Kane

Typeset at Stanford University Press in 11/16 Constantia

# CONTENTS

# FOREWORD

MARILYN YALOM was a community-maker, a bringer-together of people, a supporter of others, and a writer about the kind of friendship and love that rested at the core of her unfathomably generous heart. To all she did, she brought her particularly intense and careful way of listening, a tireless championing of others, and a delightfully mischievous sense of humor. All three are evident in the pages of this new book—a book which might come as a surprise to readers who know her only through her writing. It was in fact, at first glance, a bit of a surprise to me.

Marilyn was a feminist, early and often and wholeheartedly. She was one of the organizers and a director of what is now the Clayman Institute for Gender Research at Stanford University, "its real, on-the-ground working founder," historian Edith Gelles says, and Deborah Rhode, a subsequent director, calls her "its true leader." As the institute's director, Marilyn championed women generally and individually, bringing in visiting scholars and organizing conferences and programs to amplify female voices.

An admirer of the female-driven French salon culture of centuries past, Marilyn also hosted, with poet Diane Middlebrook, a salon of

San Francisco Bay Area women journalists, novelists, poets, nonfiction writers, and academics across all fields. Men were invited only once each year. I won't soon forget the horror I felt when, during a poetry reading at the first salon Marilyn invited me to attend, I was moved to quietly weeping among all these swanky strangers. But she invited me back, and I don't believe I launched a novel afterward without Marilyn hosting a salon to celebrate, one of the many ways she supported so many of us. Silicon Valley historian and salonnière Leslie Berlin recalls how, when she was "a lowly graduate student . . . not in Marilyn's department, in her field, or even working in the same century," Marilyn often checked in to see how her dissertation was coming and, later, was "always there with a kind word when I had something published somewhere." German-born author Renate Stendhal describes the salon as something she'd "never seen outside Europe . . . a place to call home in terms of warmth, hospitality, intellect, culture, community, writing (and baking!)."

Marilyn's prior books, too, largely focused on women. Since her 1985 debut, *Maternity, Mortality, and the Literature of Madness*, her titles alone tell us we will be reading about female lives. *Blood Sisters. A History of the Breast. A History of the Wife. The Social Sex: A History of Female Friendship. Compelled to Witness: Women's Memoirs of the French Revolution.*

In *Birth of the Chess Queen*, she explores the transformation of the sole female piece on the board, originally the game's weakest, into its strongest power. It is something Marilyn herself did in life and in her work: not just connecting us with each other—connecting women, especially—but also lifting us up.

Of course, many of these earlier books, as well as the last three published in her lifetime, are as steeped in history as is this new one. Her *The American Resting Place*, a collaboration with her photographer son, Reid, examines four hundred years of history through a look at burial grounds. *How the French Invented Love* takes readers on a journey through centuries of French literature. *The Amorous Heart* explores the heart as metaphor and icon across two thousand years.

But a collection of first-person narratives of people who were children during World War II?

Why this book? Why now?

In its final chapter, "When Memory Speaks," Marilyn tells us, "I suspect that I have written this book, long after the end of World War II, because I have carried a lifelong sense of debt to the millions who suffered instead of me. And I despair as I see how many others continue to suffer."

Here, she does what she always did so well in her writing and in life: she brings diverse elements together, and finds connection. She uses those connections to explain and explore. In exploring memories from nearly a century ago, she allows us a greater understanding of what it means to be human in this world today.

This is a Marilyn Yalom book, so have no fear: even on this literary turf of war story so often dominated by male voices, she finds space for female experience. Three pieces are written by women, including one by Marilyn herself. And the pieces by men, too, include stories of motherhood.

But more importantly, she explores that other theme of *Birth of the Chess Queen*: the conversion of weakness into strength. Here, she demonstrates that transformation through the stories of people who lived through World War II as vulnerable children and emerged to become important thinkers, teachers, and leaders. Not flawless. Not undamaged. Not without weaknesses. But ultimately strong.

In the opening memoir, "A Sheltered Vision," Marilyn considers her own childhood in Washington, DC, during the war, where "it never occurred" to her "that Jews could be a special target of attack." She ate less sugar but never went hungry. Her behavior was questioned by a teacher who frowned upon her mother working in the war effort—criticism Marilyn even as a child shrugged off, a lovely prelude to her own partnering with Irvin Yalom to raise four children while they pursued dual careers. The "innocence" of her childhood was shattered only after the war ended, when her family learned that her aunt, uncle, and cousin in Poland had died in a concentration camp. Living in France herself seven years later, she saw the lasting devastation wreaked by war.

Philippe Martial was five and had newly lost his father to paratyphoid when his family moved from the city of Djibouti in what was then French Somaliland back to his grandparents' Normandy home just before the war began. He writes in "Under German Occupation" of his experience living through the war in Fleury-sur-Andelle, near the city of Rouen which was nearly destroyed by Allied bombs. German soldiers occupied and ravaged their home. He grew up cold and hungry. His mother used burnt wood ash for soap. His is a childhood any of us would grieve to have our sons and daughters experience—yet one he is apologetic for mentioning, given what happened to others in the Holocaust.

This is a theme that surfaces in one way or another in so many of these narratives: My pain was nothing compared to that of others. My task is to channel my pain into a way to save future others who were not saved this time, but ought to have been.

"At the end of my fifth year of life," says Stina Katchadourian, "I knew two things for certain: as long as I could see Nunni at her desk writing a letter, my Papi was alive," and that clear sunny days meant night bombings. Her mother contributed her wedding ring to the Finnish war effort and received in exchange a plain iron one, which she wore "like a badge of honor, all her life." Katchadourian's story, told in "Against Two Enemies," is one of flight; her mother trying to keep her family safe in a country "squeezed between Russia and Germany" while her father commanded troops at the front. The story of how she comes to make friends in her temporary war home is among the most charming in this collection, as is the story of the send-off her teacher and classmates give her when she leaves to return home.

It is another thread that runs through so many of these stories: What is it to leave a home?

Susan Groag Bell, who was baptized in the Lutheran church but defined by German law as Jewish, fled a privileged life in Czechoslovakia for England. She traveled with her mother, believing her father would follow. In "Into Exile," she writes of waving excitedly to her father as he stood on the train station platform with her dog, never to see him again. Her war years were a challenge, spent living apart from her mother, who worked as a servant in their new life. Bell, a good student, struggled to find a comfortable place in which to learn. She settled finally into a school of Czech refugees, and returned to her home country with her classmates after the war. Her homecoming was not a success, but nor was it an easy thing to get back to England and her mother.

What is it to leave a home, only to find, on your return, that home is no longer home? That you have no place to settle? No place to become what you imagined you might be?

And what kind of society *chooses* to separate a child from her mother at such a time, or at any time?

"Within the War Machine" is one of the book's most compelling narratives—and its most disturbing. Winfried Weiss, a child of a member of the German Ordnungspolizei, the SS "green police," spent the war years haunted by a horror story he overheard: a "nest of Jews" kidnapped and killed Christian children, whose "small carcasses" were found "in a kosher butcher shop hanging from hooks like pigs and cows." Yet the end of the war is only the middle of his story. "Our capture came fast; one moment we were citizens of Hitler's Reich, and in the next we belonged to a new world," he writes. "The Americans swept in silently through the garden, surrounding us."

Marilyn shows us in her careful presentation of Weiss's narrative that, although there is evil enough in the world to wash us all in pain, the children of even the worst of us begin as innocents.

Irvin Yalom and Robert Berger's conversation in "Escaping the Nyilas" explores a friendship between two men, neither of whom can bear to talk of the Holocaust until an event in Berger's present brings back his memories. As a thirteen-year-old Hungarian Jew, he escaped a ghetto roundup and thereafter lived alone, passing as a gentile and evading exile to a concentration camp. He was fifteen when he was apprehended by a Nyilas—one of the Hungarian Nazi "militia of armed thugs who roamed the streets rounding up Jews and either killing them on the spot or taking them to their Party houses for torture and slaughter."

How heavy the burden of what we do or fail to do weighs on us, we see here. The fact that we are children doesn't save us from the guilt of our need to survive, or from the guilt of having survived.

And in "Resistance," French Ambassador and Consul General Alain Briottet remembers living in Vichy France, the child of a mother who regularly set off on her bicycle to coordinate connections between the many resistance movements, while his father was held prisoner in a German labor camp. It is a gorgeously detailed story, its ending one of the most moving moments in the book. An everyday gesture. A touch. A moment of grace that reminds us of the joy in the simple act of being together.

In connecting these stories, Marilyn bridges the gap between the child of a prominent Nazi and the niece of a victim of the Holocaust. In Germany, in Hungary, in Finland, and in Washington, DC, she shows us, a parent is to love and to be loved, yes, but also a teacher of morals, a person to admire, to learn from, to believe, to aspire to be. Right and wrong, goodness and evil, even love and hate—these are concepts defined for us as children by the adults in our lives. Concepts that, once learned, we often take unquestioned to our graves.

*Innocent Witnesses* is a call to the adults of today to challenge our certainties. To understand that what we teach today might lead to a lifetime of pain in unlearning. To see where unbending belief can lead when visited upon children unequipped to defend themselves against "patriotism," propaganda, and lies.

Marilyn explores, in the process, the nature of memory itself. Canadian author Margaret Atwood wrote in *The Handmaid's Tale*, "But who can remember pain, once it's over? All that remains of it is a shadow, not in the mind even, in the flesh. Pain marks you, but too deep to see." Memory "has its own logic," Marilyn Yalom writes here. She shares then—very near the end of the book—a story from long after the war was over, of her own mother, "in order to die peacefully," chasing an alternative memory about her sister who was murdered in the Holocaust.

Much like memory itself, this remembrance works as a sort of literary kaleidoscope through which to examine the chapters preceding it. Each memory is that of a single person. Some are steeped in research. Some are corroborated by siblings or others. Many seem simultaneously both impossible and true. It is the nature of memory: whether any detail is true is less important than the whole we carry forward, often buried so deeply that we might choose forgetting as the easier path.

But of course, we cannot forget. To forget is to allow the worst of history to happen again. To remember is both to heal and to inoculate.

And so *Innocent Witnesses* is, in the end, a call to look at the present moment, to imagine where any road might lead when it begins with separating families, closing borders, or allowing to go unchallenged the prejudice now prevalent even among the chess queens of the world's most powerful nations. These stories set in the prolonged violence of a war years past teach us how violence of any type visited on our children—drug wars in our streets, school shootings, acts of terror against people of another color or another faith—will echo through generations. It is a devastating illumination of the long-lasting impact of any moment of violence, including the one we live in today.

Yet it is also an homage to the fundamental goodness of the human spirit, and of the strength even children find at their core to carry them through. It is a life-repairing act of literary generosity, collecting and connecting diverse experiences into a narrative that is, in this particular moment in history, as necessary as it is inspiring.

MEG WAITE CLAYTON
April 2020

# PREFACE

I BELONG TO A GENERATION of people who were children during World War II. Whether living in the United States like me, or in Europe like some of the friends I acquired later in life, we all carry permanent memories of the years between 1939 and 1945. To this day, despite subsequent U.S. military interventions into Korea, Vietnam, Iraq, Afghanistan, and elsewhere, World War II remains "our" war.

This book is an effort to understand the effects of that wartime experience on children living in Europe and the United States. It is based exclusively on first-person accounts recorded by people I have known closely as adults, and on decades-long conversations with them. I could not have known these individuals when we were children during the war, but even then their experiences, as I imagined them, affected my inner world, and later I went in search of their stories.

Each of these stories presents a micro-history of World War II as filtered through a child's sensibility, and each draws us into the world of a particular child. Of course, I knew each of these wartime witnesses only as adults and must rely on their retrospective accounts as they remembered them. Yet, despite the hazards of memory, which I shall discuss in this book's epilogue, I came to trust the essence of their accounts. Children's eyes take in the everyday workings of war, and when reopened through memory, help the rest of us witness war's brutal realities.

Certainly, there have been many other books presenting the experience of wartime children. I am thinking particularly of Svetlana Alexievich's brilliant *Last Witnesses: An Oral History of the Children of World War II*, first published in Russian in 1985 but not translated into English until 2019. *Last Witnesses* is comprised of about one hundred short statements by Russian children, each remembering the cruelty of German invaders who did not spare their fathers, mothers, or even their fellow children when it suited Nazi aims. One comes away from this book with an overwhelming sense of suffering, a children's tragic chorus on an epic scale.

My book does not pretend to such dimensions. Rather, it offers a smaller number of rich, intimate accounts, through which we see deeply into the experience of children trying to grow up and understand the world around them, just as their families and countries are scrambling to survive. In addition to my own story, it offers the histories of six people whom I came to know as colleagues and friends, each of whom has written a revealing and compelling memoir. Let me introduce you to each of the authors, whose memoirs you will read in this same order.

Alain Briottet was born into a middle-class family living in Paris. His father, an educator and a reserve officer in the French army, was taken prisoner by the Germans in 1940, incarcerated in Pomerania (then part of Germany, now in Poland), and not released until 1945. Alain's memoir, *Sine Die* (published in French, Éditions Illador, 2016), describes how his family fled to a village in central France during his father's imprisonment, how his mother participated in the Resistance, and how they survived with great hardship under the collaborationist Vichy regime. A portion of his book is published here in my translation.

Philippe Martial was a young boy of five when the war started, and he spent the war years living in Normandy with his maternal grandparents. His father had died just before the start of the war, in 1939, while serving as a French army medical officer in French Somaliland. His death left his widowed wife with three small children, Philippe and his younger twin sisters. In Normandy under German occupation, they suffered the common deprivations of war—cold and hunger—and the insults of the local children, who had never seen others with dark skin and frizzy hair. Philippe's account includes memories of German soldiers billeted upon his family, terrifying bombardments, and the exhilarating liberation of the village by American soldiers. In his eighties, Philippe wrote a short memoir of the war years, which I have translated from the original French into English for this book.

Winfried Weiss was born into a modest German Catholic family from Bavaria. His father, a policeman, was a member of the Nazi party who disappeared on the Russian front in November 1943, just after Winfried's sixth birthday. Until that time, Winfried remembered a happy childhood in a community of like-minded individuals, all fully committed to Hitler, all enemies of France, Britain, and the United States, and all contemptuous of Jews. Many years after we met, I helped Winfried write and publish *A Nazi Childhood* (Capra Press, 1983 and Mosaic Press, 2010), a lyrical literary memoir deemed "shocking" when reviewed by Nobel laureate Doris Lessing. His story offers us entrée into a world that is both foreign and familiar, inviting and, yes, shocking.

Stina Katchadourian was born into the Swedish-speaking minority of Finland in 1937. Her father had a stable position in the Finnish forest industry when he was called up for military service in 1939. He spent the next six years defending Finland against Russian aggression. While her father was away, her mother moved the family around the country as far north as Lapland and then eventually to Sweden. Those turbulent years are vividly described in Stina's memoir, *The Lapp King's Daughter* (Fithian Press, 2010).

Susan Groag Bell came from an affluent family in the Czech city of Troppau. Though her parents were Jewish by birth, she had been baptized and raised as a Lutheran. This did not protect her from being dismissed from school as a Jew after the German takeover of Czechoslovakia in 1938. The following year, she fled with her mother from Czechoslovakia to England, where her mother found employment as a housekeeper and Susan was accepted gratis into a private girls' school. Her lawyer father, who stayed behind, became a victim of the Holocaust. Susan credited my "editorial pencil" with helping her to improve her account of that time, which was published as *Between Worlds: In Czechoslovakia, England, and America* (Dutton, 1991), and from which I've excerpted the narrative contained here.

Robert Berger was separated from his parents by the Nazis when he was a teenager. As a Jewish boy in Hungary posing as a Christian, he witnessed atrocities that would haunt him for the rest of his life. He and my husband, Irvin Yalom, became friends in medical school, and many years later, they co-wrote *I'm Calling the Police* (Basic Books, Kindle, 2011), which evokes the tragedies of Berger's adolescence. A shortened version of that work appears here.

Surprisingly few of these childhood stories focus exclusively on the terrors of war. As we were children, we also went on with our innocent lives, enjoying the pleasures of family and friends and routine activities. Wherever we were, we found ways to think of our situations as "normal"—at least until some overwhelming catastrophe destroyed even that illusion.

Children remember what they ate, and what they didn't eat, and especially the torments of hunger, and the selfishness of individuals who begrudged them their food. They remember the unexpected kindness of strangers who took them into their homes, and the freezing cold of unheated rooms. They remember a rare toy given to them on their birthday or at Christmas. They remember their play with other children, some of whom disappeared from their lives due to displacement or death. They remember the sound of sirens and explosions and the bright flares that illuminated the night sky.

Unlike people who were adults during the war, innocent children do not have to justify their actions in their later accounts. They were not responsible for the atrocities that war had visited upon them and on the millions of others whose lives were maimed or cut short. Rather, they were caught up in the events around them, trying to grow and discover the world during extraordinary circumstances, which often felt ordinary, if not pleasant. Reading their accounts, we learn a great deal about what it is to be human, without the lenses of geopolitical history or moral outrage through which we ourselves, looking back, might view these events.

Since their accounts were written later in their lives, the authors presented here all have an eye to the storytelling devices that compel readers. The selections I have chosen from their memoirs lay out their stories as clearly as possible, often with the child and adult perspectives intertwining to create a rich, multilayered voice that neither would offer alone.

I came to know all these children personally after they had grown up, and I have marveled at their ability to transcend the past and become thoughtful and accomplished adults. From their memoirs, it is possible to speculate on the circumstances that helped them survive. Which adult figures representing safety and hope guided them through the worst of times? What personal qualities helped them become functioning adults? How did they deal with their traumatic wartime memories? These are questions I shall address at the end of the book.

Now that several of these people have passed away and since the rest of us will undoubtedly be gone in the near future, I feel a special obligation to communicate their stories. The wartime memories conveyed in this book come from friends who spent their childhood years in France, Germany, Hungary, Czechoslovakia, England, Finland, Sweden, Norway, and the Netherlands. In addition to their recollections, I add my own wartime memories—those of an American girl safely protected in Washington, DC, while bombs dropped on my counterparts abroad.

We are the last individuals who can remember World War II, and before long we shall all vanish. I leave behind this testimonial in the hope that our stories will alert others, once more, to the senseless tragedies of war. Given the present historical moment, with its rising tide of nationalism and escalating conflicts, these stories may serve as cautionary tales, forcing us to ask whether our children and grandchildren will also be the victims of power-hungry adults. Must children continue to lose their soldier fathers and, now, their soldier mothers as well? How many will be displaced from their homelands in this age of refugees? How many will be separated from their families and placed in camps on the borders of the countries in which they seek refuge? How many will be persecuted because of their skin color? How many will be forced to suffer hunger, cold, bodily injury, and death?

INNOCENT WITNESSES

# A Sheltered Vision

*My American Girlhood and French Connection*

DECEMBER 7, 1941, "a date which will live in infamy," in President Franklin D. Roosevelt's stirring words, was supposed to be a festive day in our family. Since my mother's birthday was December 8, which fell on a Monday that year, we had planned to celebrate on Sunday, when my father's grocery store would be closed. For lunch, Mother had prepared her traditional Sunday meal of roast chicken, potatoes, and vegetables, with a special treat of homemade fudge that appealed to my sweet-toothed self. I was nine years old and my mother would be thirty-seven.

We had lunch and ate the fudge and then settled in the back room where a wooden radio four feet high awaited my father. My father's grocery store was in a distant part of town, and Sunday was the only day he was home to enjoy classical music in the afternoon.

I must have been reading one of the three books I took out each week from the Petworth Library when, at 1 p.m., a startling announcement interrupted the radio program. The Japanese had bombed Pearl Harbor. From the tone of the speaker's words, I knew that something grave had happened. But where was Pearl Harbor? And why were the Japanese involved? Weren't they the same people who had given us the lovely cherry blossoms we enjoyed every spring at the Tidal Basin?

Mother and Dad huddled around the radio for much of the afternoon, so I knew it was very, very serious. To this day, long after my

mother's death, I associate her birthday on December 8 with the trag-
edy of Pearl Harbor.

We lived in a redbrick row house at 5104 Fourth Street, NW, Washington,
DC. We had moved there in 1938, when I was six, and would remain
there until I left for college in 1950. From first through sixth grade, I
would walk the three blocks to and from Barnard Elementary School,
where my second-grade teacher wrote on my report card that I was
"pleasant, courteous, and helpful," and that my work showed "much
originality."

After school, I would hurry home to play with my friends, Janice
Reiskin from around the corner, or Doran Mitchell who lived a block
away. Janice had fat brown sausage curls and was always well-dressed
and well-mannered. I thought of her as superior to me in deportment,
though I ranked higher as a student. Doran was quite the opposite of
each of us. He was carefree at school and unruly when outside, but so
high-spirited that I always loved him in a childish way. Whenever I
could, I would stop at his house on the way home from school to see
his little twin sisters and to ingratiate myself with his mother.

My own mother was always welcoming to our friends, whether
mine or those of my two sisters, Beatrice and Lucille. Mother had
been born in London in 1904, but raised in Krakow, Poland, from
1906 until 1924, when she, her brother Alfred, her sister Ann, and her
parents emigrated to Chicago. She spoke both Polish and German as
well as English, and would sing in all three languages. Dad, who came
to the United States from Russia right after World War I, could read
Russian, Hebrew, and English, but spoke to us in English. Though
both of my parents could probably speak Yiddish, I never heard
a word of it. It was a point of honor for them to converse only in
English, so that we could all be "Americans." They even sent me
to elocution school at the age of five to polish my speech. Every

2

Saturday, for 25 cents a lesson, I learned to curtsy to Miss Betty and recite simple poems.

But there was one nearby family with whom my mother spoke German: the Steiners. They had come from Austria, and my mother had a close relationship with Mrs. Steiner. Her husband, Max Steiner, the head waiter at the Mayflower Hotel, carried himself with such dignity that I was filled with fear whenever he entered the room. But I was absolutely enchanted with their three sons, Rudy, Frankie, and Jimmy—especially Jimmy, who was two or three years older than I. With his light hair, blue eyes, and kind ways, he starred in my romantic daydreams for most of my childhood. We would go to the Steiners around Christmas to share their Christmas tree and Austrian pastries. I loved the *apfelstrudel* and *mohnkuchen* (apple strudel and poppy seed cake) and wished my mother knew how to bake them.

Because of the Steiners, I knew there were problems "overseas" even before Pearl Harbor. When I was around six or seven, I heard them repeat the German word for "crystal" followed by the word *Nacht*, which I knew from the lullaby my mother sang—"*Guten Abend, gute Nacht*" (though I had no idea what the words looked like on paper). The Steiner boys were gathered around my mother and said to her: "Don't worry. If the Germans come to America, we will protect you." I didn't understand what they were talking about. I didn't know they were referring to *Kristallnacht* when Nazis in 1938 Germany destroyed hundreds of Jewish synagogues, buildings, and shops, and arrested thousands of Jewish men. In the American community where I lived, it never occurred to me that Jews could be a special target of attack.

It was probably at Christmastime 1939 that I first heard the word *Anschluss* and became aware that Hitler had taken over the Steiners' homeland. We had seen pictures of Hitler in the newspaper and at the movie house, so all Germans took on his appearance in my mind. All I could imagine were little men with dark mustaches marching into Austrian houses much like my own. Why, then, did the Steiners and my mother want to speak German? Why didn't they just speak English like good Americans?

I never knew any black children, since schools and neighborhoods in the nation's capital were strictly segregated then. In fact, the only African Americans I ever knew were a succession of maids and the men who drove my father's grocery store truck to make deliveries at our home. Even though my father sent money to the National Association for the Advancement of Colored People and believed in "the brotherhood of man," neither he nor my mother, nor any white families we knew, had any social relations with African Americans.

I did have a deep relationship with one African American woman, Annabelle, my Aunt Esther Eig's lifelong maid. She took care of me at Aunt Esther and Uncle Sam's upscale house for a whole week when my mother was in the hospital giving birth to my younger sister Lucy. She would brush the tangles out of my hair and keep me from being teased by my older cousins, Buddy and Blaine. She didn't have to tell me to stay out of the way of my gruff Uncle Sam, who was immensely rich from his real estate dealings and cast his menacing shadow over the entire family.

We would go to the homes of our uncles and aunts for the Jewish holidays—Passover, Rosh Hashanah, Yom Kippur, and Hanukkah. This was the time for women to demonstrate their culinary skills. Aunt Frances was famous for her butter-smooth gefilte fish, accompanied by freshly ground horseradish. Aunt Adeline concocted luscious pastries: honey cakes and cookies with raspberry jam in the center. Who made those airy light matzoh balls for Passover? Certainly not my mother, who was stigmatized as the worst cook of the lot.

My favorite holiday was Halloween. Then I could dress up and be someone else: a fairy, a princess, a witch, an Austrian girl in a dirndl. I could put on lipstick and wear my mother's old hats and costume jewelry, though she never lent me her treasured Venetian mosaic beads. The boys in school reveled in their penciled-on mustaches and terrifying masks. They were pirates, ghosts, skeletons, Frankenstein monsters, but some of the boys frightened me much more without their masks. As the smallest in my class, I was careful to avoid male bullies and even some of the rougher girls.

There was one child even smaller and skinnier than I—our next-door neighbor Betsy. Betsy had real reason to know that life was unfair, since she was born with a severe birth defect in her hands. One hand had only two fingers and a thumb, while the other had a thumb, two normal fingers, and two joined together midway with the pinkie emerging from the ring finger like a Y. A year younger than I, birdlike, with big brown eyes, Betsy inspired in me a protective sense I felt for no one else. When other children taunted her with words like "three-fingered floozy," I told them it was a mean thing to do. That constituted the extent of my bravery.

My memories of those early childhood years are basically happy. I felt loved at home and well liked in school. My 1940 report card called me "a steady worker," "very enthusiastic," and "very pleasant and friendly."

I was almost ten when I entered fifth grade in February 1942. Two months earlier the United States had declared war on Japan, Germany, and Italy, and we had become allied with England and France. War would be the backdrop of my early adolescent years.

How was I personally affected by the war? Like all Americans, our family was issued a ration book. These books had stamps in them, each good for a scarce product such as sugar, butter, or meat. I remember looking at each stamp, marked with an airplane or a tank or some other image connected to the war. Because I liked sweet things very much, Mother told me that my contribution to the war effort would be to eat less sugar. I remember putting the least amount of brown sugar possible on my oatmeal and not asking my mother for a second cookie when I came home from school. I didn't care much for butter, so I did not object to the advent of margarine, then sold in its original, pasty white state, along with a glob of brownish liquid with which you mixed it to provide butter-like color.

Since my father owned a grocery store, I suspect he may have provided us with somewhat more than our share. We always had enough food, including bacon, which I loved, and canned milk, which I detested. Coffee, too, was rationed, but that didn't bother us too much since we were mainly tea drinkers. I do remember asking my dad once about the "black market." He explained to me that some dealers managed to get goods on the sly and then sold them for higher prices, but he wouldn't do that. That would not be "patriotic."

Children could be patriotic by collecting tin cans, tinfoil, and aluminum to be recycled for ammunition. I remember going out with Doran Mitchell, pulling his wagon from door to door and asking for those precious items. I also remember pasting saving stamps into war bond books that helped fund the war effort and were to be cashed in after the war. And I distinctly remember the feel of the heavy blackout curtains meant to prevent the escape of any light that might aid enemy aircraft. Having seen movies of German planes bombing England, where we had relatives, we feared the same for us.

A major change took place in our family from the winter of 1942–43 to June 1944: my mother went to work for the U.S. government! I was extremely proud that my mother was now "a government worker," even if her assignment was only to file papers. She, too, was delighted with work outside the home, allowing her for the first time in her marriage to earn money of her own. I became aware of the new niceties added to our Sunday lunches: crystal glasses and sterling silverware.

In addition to these new acquisitions, Mother acquired a new friend, her supervisor, Mrs. Chmielewski. Like my mother, Mrs. Chmielewski had been raised in Poland, and the two of them took to speaking Polish together. It was a language I very much enjoyed hearing, though the only words I understood were *I panya popolska?* (Do you speak Polish?). Since Mrs. Chmielewski had no children of her own, she doted on us. I couldn't wait for her visits when she would bring us Polish delicacies—piroshki and pastries and sometimes a scarf or ribbons for me. Now, alongside Mrs. Steiner, Mother had another Catholic friend from Europe with whom she spoke a foreign language. When I saw them together, they looked like two happy schoolgirls. But sometimes I would catch them in a sadder mood, whispering about things they didn't want me to hear. I knew it had to do with the people left behind in Poland—my mother's sister, her husband, and their daughter, who would have been about my age and who wore her hair in braids just like I did.

There was one consequence of my mother's work outside the home no one had anticipated. I was, according to my school reports of spring 1943, changing for the worse. My white-haired teacher, Mrs. Ellenor B. Whitney, wrote to my mother on April 9, 1943: "Marilyn is an enthusiastic steady worker. She is helpful and friendly at all times. She is very capable and does fine work." Then she added with a slightly darker pencil: "But I have been wondering, lately because of a change in attitude and behavior, if Marilyn is having too much freedom and being thrown too much on her own resources because you are away all day."

Whatever was going on in my life at that time—for one thing, I was much shaken up by starting my periods at the tender age of eleven—Mrs. Whitney blamed it all on my mother's work outside the home. On my report card of June 23, 1943, Mrs. Whitney continued her criticism: "She talks too much and is often too concerned about helping her neighbors, when all her attention should be given to what she has to do. She needs to quiet down."

I must have quieted down somewhat by the time I left Barnard Elementary School in February 1944, because Mrs. Whitney wrote in my autograph book in January 1944: "To Marilyn, best wishes for happiness and success. My memories of you will always be pleasant ones."

Autographs of classmates in that same book attested to the overarching presence of the war. Gloria Wallerstein appended the following ditty:

*Rubber is rationed*
*Sugar is too*
*But when it comes to sweetness*
*All I need is you.*

Ginger Wilner wrote:

*Tojo's in the kitchen*
*Spilling the beans*
*While Hitler's in the bath tub*
*Sinking submarines.*

Janice Harsh, one of my best friends, admonished, "Remember Pearl Harbor," and John Waters added, "Keep 'em flying."

In the spring of 1944, I started McFarland Junior High School, ushering in a decisive chapter in my life. With my new school farther away and my studies more demanding, I stopped coming home for lunch and started learning a new language: French. From the very first utterances by Mademoiselle Vestal, I knew that I had entered an enchanted world where mundane things like "desk" and "stairway" were transposed into magical words like *pupitre* and *escalier*. And there was the incomparable *Voilà!*, which my verbally deprived English-speaking countrymen had to do without. After a few scant weeks, I announced to my family that I was not going to be a librarian or an English teacher. I was going to teach French instead. Indeed, I stuck to that resolution for the next three decades, spending a good part of my adult life as a professor of French.

Even I knew at that time that France was occupied by the Germans and that French men and women were fighting back under the leadership of General de Gaulle. Every Saturday, we rooted for the Resistance in the newsreels shown at the neighborhood movie house. Somewhere I saw the anti-Nazi film *This Land Is Mine*, starring Charles Laughton, Maureen O'Hara, and George Sanders, and directed by Jean Renoir. It was one of the first American propaganda films featuring brave resistance fighters opposing cruel Germans, and I still remember the terrifying scene in which hostages are shot.

Our family patriotism was manifested when we took in a government worker as a boarder. With housing very scarce in Washington, DC, during the war years, my parents decided that our back room could easily be converted into a bedroom, though it would mean passing through the kitchen to get to the upstairs bathroom. Sometime late in 1944, Mrs. Harris came to live with us.

Mrs. Harris had come from the South to work for the government while her husband was away in the war. She was a big woman with lovely, powdered skin and a forceful manner. Almost immediately, she took to treating me as a young lady in need of polishing. "Come in, honey," she would say, as I stood at the kitchen door adjoining her room. As I settled into the chair by her bed, she busied herself arranging the items that struck me as wondrously glamorous: stockings and garter belts and lacy underwear.

She told me I could improve my appearance in numerous ways. If I wanted to have shiny hair, I should brush it a hundred times each day and add lemon juice when I washed it. If I wanted to have bigger breasts (mine were hardly there at all), I should stuff cotton into my bras. She would rub lotion into my hands and dab perfume behind my ears and send me off with a kiss on the cheek, as if we were girlfriends.

While millions of lives were being lost in the war abroad, I learned that one little life was growing within a person close at hand. Mrs. Harris was pregnant.

Mother announced to us at the dinner table that Mrs. Harris was going to have a baby and that she'd be looking for a new place, but that might take some time since rentals were hard to find. We girls were very excited at the thought of a baby. Could my sister Bea and I be babysitters? Despite Mother's smiling acceptance, I sensed her unease, especially after I heard her say to my dad, "How could we throw her out?"

A few months later the baby was born. I remember leaning over a metal crib against the wall in the back room and looking at a fat-cheeked ruddy infant. I liked to put my thumb in its hand and feel the instinctive grasp of miniature fingers around it. Soon Mrs. Harris was back to work, leaving her baby at a nursery center. We spent less time together, as she was constantly racing about and haggard when she came home.

Then one day everything changed. I came home to the sight of a police car parked in the front of our house. Inside, two policemen were in the living room talking to my mother. I stood in the hallway listening as they asked her about Mrs. Harris. "She's a very good mother," my mother said. "Takes very good care of the baby." No, Mother had never asked to see any identification papers. No, she didn't know exactly where Mrs. Harris worked. No, she had never met her husband . . . he was away in the war.

It seems that Mrs. Harris was not really Mrs. Harris. She was not even married. She had taken the name of a Captain Harris, who was the father of her baby, though he was married to someone else. And there was worse to come. Mrs. Harris had tried to kill Captain Harris, who, it turned out, was not away at war at all. She had arrived at his office in downtown DC with a suitcase full of lethal objects, knives and a gun among them. Threatening was as far as she got, because Captain Harris was able to disarm her and send for the police.

This sensational story appeared on the front page of the next day's *Washington Post*, with a picture of the open suitcase and its deadly contents. I was shattered, less concerned for Mrs. Harris than for myself. There was our address printed plainly in the paper for all my schoolmates to see. Our home at 5014 Fourth St., NW, had housed not only the peaceful Koenick family but also a would-be murderess. How quickly I forgot the warm and generous woman, who had tried to make a young lady out of me. Afterwards, I never tried to find out what became of her.

Only my mother, ever compassionate, felt sorry for Mrs. Harris. But my mother also had greater worries on her mind. With the war coming to an end, she was inquiring more actively about the fate of her sister, Regina, in Poland. The Red Cross assured her that they were tracking Polish Jews as best they could and would contact her as soon as they had any news. Mother became more and more anxious as the newsreels showed footage from liberated concentrations camps with stacks of bodies piled up like wood and haunting skeleton-like prisoners in striped uniforms. They were too horrifying for me to look at, and I began covering my eyes whenever they appeared. I do not remember just when Mother got the tragic news, but I do remember—I have remembered all my life—how she burst into tears and sobbed uncontrollably when she received the letter reporting the death of her sister in a concentration camp, along with her husband and daughter. I would never get to meet the cousin with braids like mine.

Just as I remember the onset of war on December 7, 1941, so, too, I clearly recall its end on August 14, 1945. I was at a girls' camp in Maryland when the bells began to ring and we heard the joyful words, "The war is over!" It was called V-J Day, shorthand for Victory over the Japanese. We girls started hugging each other and ran to the mess hall where the flag had been raised, and we began to sing: "God bless America, land that I love. Stand beside her, and guide her, Through the night with the light from above." Our counselor—I can still see her smiling face, though I have long forgotten her name—let us run around wild without her usual attention to order. At thirteen years old, I experienced a high point of happiness, shared with all my campmates, that still resonates in my octogenarian breast when I recall that exhilarating day.

It was in the fall of 1952 that I finally experienced firsthand the devastation of World War II. I was now in college, and one of my professors at Wellesley suggested that I spend my junior year in France. I jumped at the chance.

The first six weeks of my stay abroad were spent with a French family, the Quantins, in the provincial city of Tours. Even seven years after the war, there remained bombed-out areas in Tours. The ancient church near the Loire River was still partly in ruins, with stones piled up along the roadway.

I was chagrined to learn that the destruction had been caused by American bombers. Michel Quantin, the twenty-something son of the family, told me that the Americans had bombed from very great heights and would have caused less civilian damage if they had flown at lower altitudes.

"Après tout, nous étions vos alliés," he said. After all, we were your allies.

It was more common for the people of Tours to hail Americans as their saviors. One moving incident remains vividly in my mind. I was on a local bus somewhere in the countryside sitting next to a peasant woman carrying a fat hen in her lap. When she discovered that I was

Fourteen-year-old Marilyn Yalom, Washington DC, 1946.

American, she took my hand in hers and said: "Quand je pense à tous ces jeunes américains qui sont venus mourir en France pour nous. . . . " When I think of all those young Americans who came to die in France for us. . . . The French expressed gratitude on many occasions, but never more poignantly for me than on that local bus filled with peasants and their produce.

With Michel, however, the situation was more complex. In his mid-twenties, he still lived at home with his parents, having suffered a war-related breakdown in his teen years that rendered him unable to continue his studies beyond the local Jesuit high school.

Michel's mother, Madame Quantin, was one of the strangest-looking women I had ever seen. She had a paste-white face, dyed black hair, and a theatrical manner. She always wore a white jacket and a thin man's tie, a style she had adopted in the thirties when she had owned a boutique selling ladies hats. Madame Quantin had become something of a local celebrity, with a mixed reputation—it was known, for example, that Michel was not her husband's son, but the son of another man whose family were minor nobility.

She had an older son, Jean-Jacques, but Michel was clearly her favorite. He told me she had sent him to school every day with his nanny, even into his teen years, which had been deeply humiliating for an adolescent boy.

In the prewar period, the Quantin family, like many right-wing Catholics, had preferred an alliance with the Germans rather than with their mutual enemies, the Communists. This was news to me. I had no idea that some decent French people had more or less welcomed the Germans. But the people of Tours, whatever their political persuasion, soon learned that these Germans carried with them death and destruction. In June 1940, they savagely bombed Tours, leaving behind twelve acres of razed buildings, compelling the demoralized city to surrender.

Michel recalled his panic whenever he heard the sounds of war: bombs, explosions, crashes, sirens. And then there was the constant presence of German soldiers on the streets, replacing the French men, most of whom were either put in prisoner-of-war camps or sent to Germany as forced labor. It was only the comforting presence of the Jesuit priests, he said, that kept him partially sane.

You had to have known him to have appreciated his charm. Thin and dark-haired in the French manner, well-read and cultured, with exquisite manners, he reeked of refinement and neurosis. He could pour me a glass of wine with the carefree ease of a gentleman and immediately afterwards sink into boorish silence. Sometimes he was generous with his knowledge of French history and culture, at other times curt to the point of rudeness. I always wondered how much of his neurosis was related to his wartime experiences, how much to his bizarre mother and ambiguous paternity, and how much just to genetic predisposition.

I spent the rest of the school year in Paris, domiciled with another American girl, chez Madame Dubois at 96 Avénue Kléber in the chic 16th district. There, in an *ancien régime* atmosphere of Louis XVI furniture and fine engravings, it seemed as if there never had been a war. Yet a few remnants of wartime shortages remained. Only one small furnace provided heat for all the rooms and another contraption heated the water in the bathroom. My roommate and I were allowed only one bath per week. Butter was still in short supply, so we were asked to use it sparingly. And a black market thrived in foreign currency. Shamefully, I admit to having used it whenever my funds ran low, since American dollars exchanged on the black market got a higher rate than when exchanged legally.

I took courses on contemporary French literature at the Sorbonne and medieval sculpture at the Louvre and spent my weekends imbibing culture. It was the heyday of existentialism, and the Latin Quarter where I studied was its home. We looked for Jean-Paul Sartre and Simone de Beauvoir at their known hangouts in the cafés of Saint-Germain-des-Prés, but we never saw them. However, I did see the initial production of Samuel Beckett's *Waiting for Godot* and had no trouble recognizing existentialist despair, even when packaged in the garb of vaudeville comedy. It was obvious that "Godot" stood for "little God," and that God was never going to come. The war had engendered an intellectual climate that questioned the value of many traditional French institutions, such as the Church, and argued that life was, at best, "absurd." It would be many more years before the French began to look at their wartime experiences more factually.

Although I studied at the Sorbonne and the Louvre alongside French students, it was difficult to meet them outside of class. They were simply not very friendly to foreigners. Instead, I got to know a group of Norwegian students. There was a young man, Halvor, in my literature course. He had curly red hair, green eyes, and the unwashed smell we Americans never got used to. I invited Halvor to a party at our apartment, and he came with several friends, who lined up at the door and entered with a polite bow, each carefully pronouncing his name: Halvor, Lars, Tor, Olaf. They all spoke outstanding French, as well as impeccable English. Olaf, the tallest, had clear blue eyes and blond hair like corn silk. He was studying at Sciences Po and was to become my Paris boyfriend.

A few years older than I, Olaf had lived the war years under German occupation. He was eleven or twelve in the spring of 1940 when the Germans invaded Norway. Coming from a fine family that included the well-known linguist Olaf Broch, for whom he had been named, Olaf remembered the war as a time of deprivation and sorrow. As a growing boy—he eventually reached the height of six foot four—Olaf

Twenty-one-year-old Marilyn Yalom discovering Paris during her
junior year abroad from Wellesley College, 1953.

said he was always hungry. There just hadn't been enough food, even though his family had started raising their own vegetables and keeping some small animals right in the city of Oslo.

He remembered his family's disdain for collaborators with the Nazis, beginning with the infamous Vidkun Quisling, prime minister of the Nazi's puppet regime in Norway. He remembered his family's support for King Haakon, who had courageously resisted the German take-over of Norway, and their sigh of relief when it was reported that the King and the Crown Prince had safely escaped to England. He still bore a grudge against the neighboring Swedes, whom he referred to as "the Germans of the North." The Swedish royal family had shown sympathy for the Nazis, in part because the Queen was of German origin, but also because they wanted to ward off German aggression and remain neutral during the war. Olaf did not give Sweden full credit for taking in displaced refugees, including a group of highly threatened Jews from Denmark.

He was proud of the many Norwegians who had been part of an organized, highly successful resistance against the Nazis, but was ashamed of the many Norwegian women who had had relations with German soldiers. After the war, those women, known as "German girls," were stripped of their Norwegian citizenship and deported, along with their children, to Germany. As I was writing this section in October 2018, seventy-three years after the end of the war, my morning newspaper told me that the Norwegian government had just offered an official apology to those "German girls."

French women known to have consorted with German soldiers were also penalized after the war. As many as 20,000 suffered the indignity of having their heads shaved in public and of being paraded around in trucks for public revilement. I saw pictures of them in newsreels and magazines, and photos of other "traitors" brought to justice, sometimes violently. As often happens, women were the easiest scapegoats for the shame of collaboration with the enemy, the details of which would not be fully revealed until several decades after the war.

In spite of those infamous examples, the French could claim that a large part of their Jewish population had not perished; the latest estimates of total Jewish survival in France are as high as 75 percent. Many Jewish children were hidden in convents and families, including two of my adult friends, Marguerite Lederberg and Nellie Langmuir, who were taken in by Christian families who passed the children off as their own. A provincial Catholic family risked their lives by harboring Nellie and her sister, both old enough to understand the perils they were facing. In the case of Marguerite, who spent the war years in a Protestant family near Cognac while her parents were in the Resistance, she did not know that she was Jewish until the war had ended and her parents came to retrieve her.

Tragically, this was not the case for many other Jewish children. Right after the war, my friend Howard Epstein found himself in Paris renting a room that had belonged to a Jewish girl before she had been deported and killed. Because of his lifelong concern for her and for others with the same fate, he became one of the editors of the American edition of *French Children of the Holocaust* (New York University Press, 1996), written originally in French by Serge Klarsfeld to document the deaths of Jewish children in France. Klarsfeld, himself a Jewish survivor of the Nazi occupation, spent decades compiling the hefty tome of 1,881 pages that chronicles the lives and deaths of 11,402 Jewish girls and boys rounded up by French and German authorities from 1942 to 1944 and deported to Auschwitz and other death camps. Of these children, approximately 300 survived. Klarsfeld's memorial to the murdered Jewish children, replete with 2,500 photos, is testimony to the monstrous evil perpetrated not only by the occupying Germans but also by their French collaborators. Those children did not live to tell their wartime tales.

Long after the war, the French slowly acknowledged the role played by many of their compatriots in the deportation of French Jews and other Jews without French citizenship. They also grudgingly acknowledged the importance of the Communists in the Resistance, although they emphasized the primacy of General de Gaulle and his followers. But in 1952–53 when I first went abroad, few of the French people I knew wanted to talk about the war. Their memories were too painful and, in some cases, tinged with guilt. Far from what we Americans had been led to believe, many French men and women had tacitly accepted the German occupation and many others supported the collaborationist regime headed by Marshal Pétain. It was many years before I came to know French men and women willing to share with me their honest wartime memories.

Among my European friends who experienced the war at close range, the French come first in this study, because of my lengthy connection with France and also because of my access to the exceptional sources presented in the next two chapters: the first written by Alain Briottet, the second by Philippe Martial. Both Briottet and Martial suffered from the absence of their fathers, one having died immediately prior to the war while serving as an army doctor and the other held prisoner by the Germans for almost six years. Both boys spent the greater part of the war with their mother and siblings in rural settings inhabited mainly by peasants and other non-bourgeois provincials. Both knew the deprivations wrought by hunger, cold, and displacement from their homes. Both suffered the ravages wrought by German soldiers and the bombardments inflicted by the Allies. Yet the differences in their experiences are also considerable. Their narratives reveal how two boys, with somewhat similar class histories, can emerge with very different views. For Philippe, the war was a total disaster and the French had little to be proud of. For Alain, too, the war was a total disaster, but some of the French, including his mother, acted heroically. As a pair, these two stories of daily life during the German occupation both reflect and contradict each other.

# CHAPTER TWO

# Resistance

*Inside France's "Free Zone"*

**Alain Briottet** was only two when his father, a reserve officer in the French army, was called to duty. M. Briottet was captured by the Germans at the Battle of Dunkirk, June 4, 1939, and spent the next five years shuffled between various prisoner of war camps in Pomerania, a region of northern Germany bordering the Baltic Sea. Alain was seven when his father returned home, and his father's absence during those formative years would mark the young Briottet for his entire life.

Alain Briottet's mother moved her family of three—Alain and his older sister and brother—from Paris, occupied by the Germans, to the *zone libre*, controlled by Marshal Philippe Pétain's Vichy government, in 1941. They went with great hope. "We never doubted," he writes, that the "young, impatient Resistance of Limousin which people were whispering about at the beginning of 1941, would grow considerably, and play an enormous role in fighting against the occupation."

His memoir, *Sine Die*, long sections of which I have translated here, was published in 2016.

DURING THE FIRST MONTHS of the German occupation, everything conspired to make our life in Paris more arduous and more difficult. At night, there were the first British bombardments of the capital. The strident screams of sirens announcing the bombardments came to wake us from our already troubled sleep. Equipped with our pathetic gas masks, we went down quickly into the cellar, which had been transformed into an underground shelter. We waited in the dark, seated on boards that had been hastily transformed into benches, breathing the dust of the earth rancid from rat droppings and the sour odor of the sewers. We anxiously waited for the sirens that signaled the end of that alert or the beginning of something worse.

With the heat cut off in our building, we began to suffer from the cold. Like many Parisians, we often spent the afternoon in the Metro to warm up a bit. We suffered even more from hunger. Provided with our ration cards, my brother was willing to wait in the long lines in front of the grocery stores. Exchanging our coupons carefully, he tried to bring home some milk, some bread, some potatoes. The small officer's pay that my mother received (in his prisoner camp, my father hardly kept anything for himself) did not permit us to resort to the black market, which didn't take long to develop in the capital. With money, you could find everything. After paying the rent for the apartment, there wasn't much left of my father's pay to cover the daily life of four people. My mother sacrificed a great deal for us: she was getting very thin, she ate very little. She began to think that moving to the country would allow us to live better with little money. At the beginning of the winter of 1941, my mother decided to leave Paris and to relocate in La Creuse (a district in the *zone libre*, or "free zone"; while the north of France, including Paris, was under direct German occupation, the *zone libre* in the south was ostensibly controlled by the French themselves.)

The *zone libre*. At my age, it was difficult to understand what it meant, but it seemed to me nonetheless like the place where there would no longer be German soldiers to threaten us, to arrest us, maybe to kill us, or even more terrible, to separate us.

The *zone libre*—my mother repeated that term frequently, and never said "the southern zone." She seemed to grab onto the word *libre*, free. In her mouth, *zone libre* had a happy resonance, as if it designated the country where we would no longer be unhappy, the country where we would no longer be fearful, the country where we would eat as much as we wanted, the country where we would remain together.

Young Alain Briottet (center), sitting with his mother, siblings,
and cousin in La Creuse, 1942.

The free zone was opening up before us.

At that moment, we didn't imagine that it could disappear so brutally,
and that tranquility and the semblance of peace would not last for long.

At that moment, we could not have imagined that we were headed
toward a destination that was more dangerous than that we'd left behind, that we were taking refuge in a little village that would be even
more threatened than the great city that my mother had worked so
hard to get us out of. We could not imagine that, in the fury of the last
months of the war, La Creuse would be spattered with so much blood.

Throughout the war, it was a point of honor for my mother to always dress
with care. She never would have gone out of the house, even for shopping

or going to the post office, with a run in her stocking. She never would have gone out in the city without her gloves, usually leather or netting according to the season, or without her purse, a large black leather bag with a big gilded buckle, the symbol of past wealth which she still carried to hold her money and identity papers. Before we had left for the *zone libre*, my mother had pinned on her suit jacket a brooch which she thought of as a good luck charm, a brooch which my father had given her at the time of their engagement, a silver sea horse with blue stones for its large eyes. This marine animal didn't seem very beautiful to me, but my mother endowed it with mysterious, beneficial powers.

My mother took risks without thinking too much about the consequences. Shortly after our arrival in La Creuse my mother began to coordinate connections between the many resistance movements which were being formed, often in opposition to one another. She did so on her bicycle, often without considering the dangers. The Resistance leaders, both Communist and Gaullist, disagreed on numerous points: on the means to be employed, on the conduct of the war, on postwar organization. They fought bitterly over leadership in the region, but the Communists quickly won out. None of this made the jobs of less prominent members of the Resistance any easier. Asked to transport tracts or newspapers, those anonymous resisters remained in the shadow, limiting themselves to following orders and fulfilling their missions, which were often very modest but nonetheless dangerous.

As for my mother and the majority of French men and women, to resist was a natural reaction, free and disinterested, pure and spontaneous, beyond politics. Regardless of Marshal Pétain, France could not become German. The victor of Verdun could not accept such a destiny for France. Like many French people, my mother believed that Pétain was resisting in his own way, that he was playing a double game. It wasn't very dignified, nor very glorious, but one could accept it. She lost her illusions the moment that Marshal Pétain publicly announced his collaboration with Nazi Germany. The demise of the *zone libre*, in November of 1943, ultimately convinced her, and her resistance to the occupier intensified.

Toward the end of the month of July 1940, the International Red Cross officially confirmed to my mother that my father was being held in the camp of Gross-Born in Pomerania. They indicated that he was in good health. We could write him at the address written on their carte-lettre and send him packages through them. From that moment on, my mother manifested an almost blind confidence in the International Red Cross, which was, at least at the beginning of the war, the only important organization that concerned itself concretely and regularly with prisoners of war.

Later, after his return from Germany, my father emphasized the care with which the Red Cross put together its packages and the regularity of their delivery. He waited for them, impatiently, because of the shaving soap which was rarely forgotten. Sometimes, to his great joy, there were two packages of Nestlé sweetened condensed milk, and a few squares of chocolate.

The packages Mother had sent him were much poorer, but once we had arrived in La Creuse, she was able to improve them somewhat. Our village didn't have too many resources. Mainly, she put in food produced by our modest farms: salted pork, cheese, that cheese from La Creuse which is harder than stone, dried nuts, apples, very small apples with an acid taste, that she wrapped up in newspaper, sometimes a pot of honey. She added some ersatz coffee and a few lumps of sugar taken from our minuscule rations, and some underwear, shirts and t-shirts bought from neighbors, some woolens, socks, sweaters, knitted at home.

From my father's letters, she realized that the dilapidated state of the soldiers' clothing constituted a daily form of suffering, one that became especially difficult to endure when the punishing cold weather arrived. The officers, taken prisoner in June, were wearing their summer uniforms, and of course, they didn't have any luggage.

The packages which their families and the Red Cross sent them made the situation a little better. But the problem of their socks remained throughout their interment. Neither France nor Germany kept up with the need for socks. They wear out easily in countries which have snow, especially for men condemned to long obligatory marches.

The lack of books distressed my mother. My father reassured her that his Parisian comrades, who were omnivorous readers—some read as many as three or four books a week, if not more—received a quantity of them from their wives living in cities or from diverse associations established to aid prisoners. With the arrival of all those books, a library was created in Gross-Born, in spite of the German censure, focused mainly on Anglo-Saxon literature. Nonetheless, *Gone with the Wind* managed to pass through the barbed wire.

As for packages "from Pétain," which prisoners received on special occasions and most notably for Christmas, my father was a little ashamed to accept them, of letting his stomach take charge. But dying from hunger, a hunger intensified and rendered unbearable by the Pomeranian winter, he chewed the biscuits sent by Marshal Pétain ravenously. To relieve his conscience, he and his comrades, who disliked Pétain as much as he did, burned countless photos of the French chief of state and all the propaganda brochures in the large stove of their room.

I watched my mother put together her packages on the dining room table. She concentrated completely on what she was doing and was thus totally indifferent to my presence. I watched her wrap up each item, with a strip of well-worn sheet or an old newspaper, each piece with infinite care. I watched her place all these little packages in a large box, pack them down, wedge them in with little pieces of carefully folded cardboard, and sometimes start all over again so as to adjust them better and not lose any room. I watched her close the box with a large string and make several twists before tying it. I watched her fill out applications and labels, with pen and ink, using the tall, slanted writing of young ladies from the Sacred Heart, labels which, to finish the process, she had to stick on the sides of the box.

Did I experience jealousy in the face of all the attention paid to this man, my father, whom I did not know? Could one experience jealousy toward this distant person whom we invoked in our prayers? Could one experience vile and lowly feelings toward the one who ended his letters with these words: "Above all, don't deprive yourself of anything for me." Letters read to us by my mother, often in tears. This abstract figure, this respected and sacred entity, "The Prisoner," who was embodied for me only in the photo standing on the table next to my mother's bed, a photo which I looked at now and then with a furtive and fearful eye.

At the beginning of the month of December 1942—my father had already arrived in Arnswalde—my mother wanted to mark the next celebration of Christmas and give a little more luster to her packages. She had the idea of adding a large photo showing us in ceremonial dress. She decided to take us to a professional photographer in Limoges. Further away than Monluçon, Limoges—only recently occupied by the Germans—was an even larger city with numerous stores. It was quite an expedition, which took us three days because there were few connections between the two bordering departments, La Creuse and La Haute-Vienne. It was an expedition which my mother conducted with her habitual vigor and tenacity.

At Limoges, we spent the night in a hotel, my first hotel night. It was a marvelous moment for me, habituated as I was to more rusticity in our village, where there was no running water or electrical cables, and where we had to go to the well with heavy wooden buckets to fetch water. The old hotel elevator decorated with a big vertical mirror where you could see yourself from head to toe, the toilet flush with its chain furnished with a porcelain handle, the bell, all these arrangements, all these objects, constituted for me ever so many astonishing discoveries. I experimented with them one by one, like a little Lord Fauntleroy, with the sole goal of seeing the effect they produced, which occasioned a certain emotion in this tranquil provincial hotel, relatively untroubled by the war. In the morning, they brought us our breakfast in our room, on a pretty set of dishes decorated with little flowers, but the portions of butter and jam seemed very skimpy and the coffee had a strange taste. They carried down our bags, I should say our one bag. Things were done as they had been before the war.

The photographer understood that he had to make a reassuring image, comforting, elegant. Still, the photo had something unreal about it. We seemed more constrained yet serene, our faces very smooth, apparently well nourished, our look very calm, as if we were living a comfortable life in a country at peace. My father would be proud to show his comrades this photo of a beautiful and distinguished woman, surrounded by handsome children, his children.

With the landing of the Allied Forces on June 10, 1944, the Germans became more desperate and more vindictive. While the SS "Das Reich" division was coming dangerously close to our village, without our knowing anything, without our even suspecting that we were threatened, one morning in the last weeks of May my mother discovered within the high damp grass the white canvas of a parachute left there during the night. The Allies, a few weeks before the landing, had begun to drop arms and flares by parachute into the interior of the country. Footsteps marked the damp humid grass, but the aviator, surely an RAF pilot, had disappeared. Under the rising sun, the beautiful immaculate sail radiated light. My mother remained taken aback for a moment, then she seized and folded it. She thought for a moment about burning it—she had to leave no trace, in case the Germans came as far our village—but she decided against it: a fire would alarm the neighboring farms.

Instead, she folded it into a package, as flat as possible, and hid it under the big rocks of the little wall that surrounded the oak grove. She couldn't bring herself to destroy this signal, which she had been impatiently anticipating for months, like all the other resisters in the interior of the country. Having come from the sky, it restored her hope and courage, it encouraged her to become even more audacious, it announced that the landing was coming very soon, that it was only a question of the day, that the Allies were going to succeed, and that our resurrection would begin. Our resurrection would happen all at once, as all resurrections do, it would spring up, supernaturally, luminous, and without a hitch, putting an immediate end to the war. My mother's faith was already very great, but the war had reinforced and multiplied it. Facing danger, she turned to "her saints"—the little nun from Lisieux and the carpenter of Nazareth were her favorites. Or she sang. She sang arias from opera, popular romance songs, and songs heard on the radio.

At that moment, could she possibly have thought that the Allies' extraordinary enterprise would provoke, in a forgotten region of France, a terrible and unexpected reaction from the Germans? War would appear, here, as if by surprise. It would surge up far from the front and the strategic axes, in this abandoned countryside without energy or material resources. The irreparable would be committed far from the beaches of the landing, but so close to our village, so close to our house, so close to us.

In the hours that followed, we learned about the massacre at Oradour-sur-Glane. At the end of the day, a witness broke the news. An entire village of 642 people had been massacred. The women and children were locked in the church, and when they tried to escape, they were met with machine gun fire: 247 women and 205 children were killed. The men were led to six barns and sheds, machine gunned, covered with fuel, and then set on fire. This infamous massacre was the work of the 2nd SS Panzer Division, "Das Reich," under the direction of SS-Sturmbannführer Adolf Diekmann.

While Oradour was still burning and fire was reddening the sky, a resister from Limoges telephoned the village post office to relate what had happened. A young boy who went from commune to neighboring commune to announce the terrible news came quickly to our house by bicycle. He took us by surprise while we were at the dinner table. Seeing my mother's horrified face in response to his anguished words, I understood, in spite of my young age (I was little more than six), the horror and the amplitude of the disaster. I felt that, once again, danger was descending upon us.

A little later, the FTP, Francs-Tireurs et Partisans, confirmed the terrifying slaughter, unmasking the unspeakable.

On their side, the Germans tried to impose silence on the terrified population, the silence of terror, the silence of death.

The departments of La Haute-Vienne d'Oradour-sur-Glane and La Creuse bordered each other. The clear and peaceful waters of the Creuse joined those of the Vienne. For centuries, since the Hundred Years War, since the Wars of Religion, nothing had come to trouble their flow, nor their banks which had appeared so gentle to the eyes of artists, and no blood had reddened the water.

Suddenly our refuge no longer existed.

The news from Paris gave us confidence. Friday, August 25, 1944, Paris was liberated. General de Gaulle arrived at night. The next day, Saturday the 26th, he descended the Champs-Elysées, swept forward by a giant human tide. When he reached Notre Dame, the welcoming shots from the rooftops provided an ultimate, gripping echo. In the nave, he advanced in a solemn manner, each step calm and slow. The archbishop-cardinal who had escorted Marshal Pétain there several months earlier was asked not to appear. The gunshots resonated again in the cathedral, without piercing the voices of the Magnificat. Under such circumstances, "The irreproachable spire of Notre-Dame," as the poet Péguy wrote, "could not fail."

In La Creuse, we regained our strength, we had to hold out for another year.

The war didn't end up ending.

From D-Day to the German surrender, we had to endure nearly a year until May 1945. Moreover, we had to experience a new form of burial under the snow in the winter of 1944–45.

For several months, the uncertainty concerning my father continued to grow. I didn't really understand the anxiety surrounding us, which manifested itself more and more through my mother. I could read it on her face and sense it in her agitation, because she was never still. She seemed to be always on the watch, looking through the window for the arrival of the postman, waiting for a letter, a notice from the post office, a letter from the International Red Cross.

We didn't have a telephone, neither did anyone else in the village. We had to go to the post office in town to use the telephone.

In Paris and in the big provincial cities, the telephone helped people endure the anxiety of waiting. Prisoners' wives could contact their loved ones, exchange information, call the Red Cross offices, the centers of aid, and get news from foreign administrations and embassies. They could find out where the first repatriated prisoners would be assembled, learn their itinerary, and the date of their return. In our village in La Creuse, the isolation which had provided protection—which we had so obstinately searched out and obtained with so much difficulty—now added to our disquiet.

At the end of winter, it must have been around the end of April 1945, my mother received a precursory sign from Geneva—a telegram from the International Red Cross.

The telegram said that my father had just been liberated and that he was in the camp of Wietzendorf in Lower Saxony. But the telegram didn't say anything about the date of his repatriation, nor the conditions of his return, nor the state of his health. From that moment on, my mother started bicycling again.

She decided to go every day to the train station in Giat, in Puy-de-Dôme, the station nearest our village, to wait for the evening train from Paris, which carried groups of prisoners.

She wanted to be on the return *quai*, just as she had been on the departure *quai* at the Gare de l'Est on a certain day in the month of September 1939, when they had said good-bye.

In the month of May 1945, she felt that her place was there, on the *quai* of that little train station in Puy-de-Dôme, and that she should be the first to greet him. And since my father was not among those who arrived, she asked all those men who were coming out of packed compartments, crazy with joy, impatient to fall into the arms of loved ones, but they didn't know how to answer. Some of them cried out from the open doors of the train which was already moving ahead to other destinations: "Wait, wait, other trains will arrive."

My mother left every day late in the afternoon, once we had returned from school, and she did not come back till very late at night. She covered more than forty kilometers by bicycle. She said that the long trips back and forth didn't tire her out, and that, on the contrary, they calmed her nerves and impatience. She said that on the return, she liked to smell the perfume of the fields and that the cool evening air refreshed her. She wasn't afraid of passing through fields and taking dangerous roads far from any habitation in a region which the end of the war had torn apart and delivered to bloody purification.

The resisters, the *francs-tireurs*, the *maquisards*, the partisans of Georges Guingouin, "the resisters of the twenty-fifth hour," sought out "collaborators," "Vichyists," "profiters from the black market," to get revenge. The number of arbitrary arrests, of summary executions, of imprisoned women, of women whose heads were shaved, of women who were raped in the most bestial manner, continued to rise. In this "purification," women were, in numerous cases, the scapegoats. They had to expiate, not only their own sins but also those of the men. Sins that were certainly pardonable compared to the men's.

In the course of the months of April and May 1945, everything accelerated. After the entry of the Red Army into Berlin and Hitler's suicide on April 30, Germany signaled, on May 8, its unconditional capitulation on all the fronts.

Our happiness, such as it was, centered entirely on the love that our mother felt for us, and which we returned just as intensely; we didn't know any other, and I believe that neither my sister nor I wanted any other. For my brother, it was different; he was no longer a child. His school and internship had made him tough. The *maquis*, Resistance fighters, had pushed him prematurely into adulthood and into the world of men. He had seized his independence, continued to affirm it, and would never go backwards.

Our village had been the miraculous place for our happiness, where we had thrived in spite of recent trials and suffering. We could not believe that we would be destined to leave it with a definitive good-bye. The beautiful, wild nature which surrounded it and protected us had helped us live, grow, and become who we were.

One night, my mother heard the throbbing of a car motor, which seemed to have stopped in front of the house. She got up and ran to the window. In the car headlights, she saw two men who had gotten out and were looking at the silent facade. She immediately recognized my father by his silhouette, a thin and young silhouette. He wasn't yet forty. He wore a long coat thrown across his shoulders.

From the window she cried out, shouted his name, and ran out to meet him, in the nightclothes she was wearing, without taking the time to put anything on her back, with bare feet and her hair undone.

Facing my father, facing her husband whom she had not seen for almost six years, she took his head in her hands and looked at it, as close as possible for a long time without saying anything, as if she were looking to find his features, those she had known and which had remained in her memory, those she perhaps feared to have lost after such a long absence. Curiously, absence blurs in our minds our memory of features of beloved faces more than the memories they have left with us.

She inclined his head to the right, then to the left, as if she wanted to verify that his head was intact and still worked. But when she passed her hand across his face, slowly, softly, she felt that his traits had acquired folds, that deep wrinkles lined his forehead, that his hair had fallen out, as well as several of his teeth. Looking into his eyes, she saw that tears were falling. Hugging him close to her in her arms, touching him, pressing him with her fingers, she felt the bones sticking out of his skinny body. His whole body floated in his clothes.

But he was smiling.

He could not express himself in any other way. He could not speak. No sound, no speech, no word came from his mouth. He smiled to say that he was still alive, that he had endured, that he had managed to come back to us. He smiled to excuse his poor appearance, his tattered, worn-out clothes, his skinny body; to excuse his weathered face, and the tears he could not hold back. He cried with joy to have found us again. He cried for fear that we would not recognize him.

All those tears he had held back in the camps, he could now let them flow.

# CHAPTER THREE

# Under German Occupation

*The Brutal Winters of Normandy*

***Philippe Martial*** was born in Indochina in 1934, where his father was a doctor in the military. After several years there, and in French Somaliland, where his father died, he returned to France with his mother and sisters, just as the war was breaking out. They lived through the war in Normandy, which was occupied by the Germans. Philippe's interest in letters, history, and art was evident from a young age, as was his sharp, inquisitive mind.

During the forty years that I have known Philippe, I have regularly been the recipient of his generosity, his old-style courtesy, and his vast cultural knowledge. I have often asked Philippe about his childhood during World War II, and he obliged me with so many stories that I began to feel a personal connection with his past. He recently wrote a short memoir, which I translate from the French here.

MY FATHER CAME FROM FRENCH GUIANA to study medicine in Bordeaux in 1920, and subsequently became an officer in the Overseas Division of the French Army; being a quarter black, he thought he might experience less racism working in the outer colonies. After years of medical service, he was on leave in Paris when he married the daughter of commander Henri Brinkert. Despite the fact that he was black, her family put aside their prejudices and accepted the distinguished captain into the family.

My father continued his military career as a doctor in Indochina— then a French colony consisting of today's Vietnam, Laos, and

Cambodia—in the Lanson Hospital north of Tonkin, where I was born in 1934. My twin sisters arrived eighteen months later.

We spent only three years there, but the experience made my father extremely critical of colonial administration. He viewed the bureaucrats as mostly racists, who sought only to extract maximum profits by exploiting the indigenous people. In 1934, he predicted: "If France continues in this fashion, she'll lose Indochina, and then she'll lose Algeria as well." No one wanted to listen to his warnings.

My father was promoted to Chief of Health Services in French Somaliland, and we moved to the city of Djibouti. His mission was to expand and modernize its hospital. Situated on the equator, Djibouti has a punishing climate. Quickly worn out by work and the weather, my father contracted paratyphoid and died suddenly on June 18, 1939, at the age of forty-four.

Our family returned to France and took refuge with my grandparents in a large house they had rented in the village of Fleury-sur-Andelle, located in Normandy twenty kilometers from Rouen. The building was referred to locally as a *château* because it had a dovecote, an old pigeon house, which was an ancient sign of nobility, but it was little more than a large country house. We had barely moved in when war was declared against Germany on September 9, 1939, less than three months after my father's death. I had just turned five.

In the beginning, during the so-called phony war, the eight months leading up to outright warfare with the Germans, calm reigned in the village of Fleury-sur-Andelle. One day, my grandmother found me scribbling away. I dreamed of receiving mail like the adults and was trying to imitate the mysterious signs of writing. She patiently taught me the alphabet, so I already knew my letters when I started school in October 1939. My mother, with her social prejudices, had enrolled me in a private school. God forbid we should go to the public school with the village urchins! Not with them! Madame Tocqueville was both the school's director and the only teacher. She was extremely religious. Each day, the lessons began with the Lord's Prayer and a prayer to the Virgin Mary. At Christmas, I remember, each of us three children received a bicycle, and we raced about like crazy on the garden paths.

In April 1940, the military debacle began. Even our grandfather, a former commandant, was called up to the front. Our anxiety increased. The first signs of the approaching war terrified us: our neighboring village, Charleval, was bombarded. What would happen to Fleury?

In June 1940, with the Germans getting closer, my mother decided to flee the village. She rented a car and the five of us, including our grandmother, took off on the route leading west. I have no memory of the trials which marked our journey, except that we kept moving west, as far as the Vendée region, where we found refuge in the Château de Saint-Florent-des-Bois, near the town of La Roche-sur-Yon. The chateau belonged to the Countess of Clé, who greeted us when we arrived and helped install us in a long building flanked with a neo-gothic chapel. There was no running water and no electricity; it was lit with acetylene lamps.

During that sinister period, I impatiently awaited the 12th of August, my birthday. I would be six years old. I looked forward to a little party, and I knew a cake was in the making. Alas, the morning of my birthday, I was seized with a heavy fever, one that marked the beginning of a long series of medical and psychosomatic illnesses, always at the worst of times, that ruined my happiness. The doctor diagnosed paratyphoid—the same sickness that had killed my father. Soon afterwards, my sister Claudine was stricken with the same illness. Fortunately, we both recovered.

After several months, a friend wrote from Fleury-sur-Andelle, urging us to come back as soon as possible. Right after our departure,

Five-year-old Philippe Martial in Fleury-sur-Andelle, proudly wearing
the cross of honor from his school, 1940.

the Nazis had arrived and, discovering our large house empty, they moved in and used it as garrison headquarters. Occupied and ravaged by German troops, our house was becoming uninhabitable: none of the doors and windows remained intact.

I was six years old. The ignorant child I had been was changing, and I had begun to understand some of the horrors of war. Returning to Fleury, I saw firsthand the brutal stupidity of the human beasts who had destroyed our home.

The military had given free rein to their habitual savagery. They had pillaged and carried off anything that intrigued them. Gifts given to my father in Djibouti from former patients—a sumptuous carpet, mementos of silver, ivory, and lacquer—were carried off to Germany. Anything not stolen was vandalized. My grandparents' furniture was thrown into the fireplace and burned. The Germans burned the display case full of the objects our family had brought back from Indochina, tearing off the hinges, and digging out the stone incrustations from the lacquered cabinet. For good measure, they shot a bullet into the bell of a pagoda.

My mother was furious for years, and would often say: "I hope that bombs have destroyed everything the Boches (a nasty word for Germans) stole from me." And I would reply: "I hope that everything has been carefully preserved in a German family." Then I'd add: "We are never the owners of a work of art, we are only its temporary caretakers."

The child I had been later came to understand that in a time rampant with the worst massacres, the destruction of a home and the loss of furniture was nothing. What are material concerns next to the Shoah?

The house was uninhabitable, and my grandparents rented a house with a garden near the center of town. The mayor of Fleury knew that my mother spoke German, so he asked her to act as an interpreter whenever there was litigation between villagers and German officers of the occupying troops. I did not understand everything my mother reported to her parents each evening, but I listened carefully and retained snatches of conversation. Judging from what they said, I came to feel that many people were behaving dishonorably and that there was nothing to be proud of in being French.

Like most of the bourgeoisie, my mother's family supported Marshal Pétain. From 1918 to 1940, Pétain was considered "the illustrious victor" of World War I, and in June 1940, when the country was divided into the German-occupied north and the "free zone" in the south, he became the "savior." The bourgeoisie was ferociously conservative, and on the whole, shared the popular belief that "a German occupation is better than victory for the Bolsheviks."

Even the press was unfavorable to the Soviets and closed its eyes to Hitler's monstrosities. I have a horrible, tenacious memory of an atrocious newspaper photo that presented the Soviets in their worst light: it showed Finnish bodies, massacred by the Russian army, piled up in a cellar.

At Madame Tocqueville's deeply religious school, I was taught that Jews were bad people, that they belonged to a race of deicides. They had killed God when they crucified Jesus! Two thousand years later, it was considered a sacred duty to hold a grudge against such brigands. And the propaganda! It held sway on walls with posters that told you how to recognize a Jew. The caricatural design was always in profile, with an exaggerated nose, considered typical of the race.

Under Pétain, anti-Semitism became quasi-official. One of the first acts of the Pétain government was to forbid Jews to cross the line of demarcation between the north and the south. The laws of October 18, 1940, and June 2, 1941, closed off certain occupations to Jews. Finally, the high point of ignominy came on July 16, 1942, when the government facilitated the roundup of 13,000 Jews, including 5,000 children, who were crammed into the Vel d'Hiv, a sports stadium, and then deported to the gas chambers.

Fortunately, in our village these ideological efforts were blunted by a certain inertia. Fleury-sur-Andelle had two doctors, one of whom was Jewish. In all probability, many of the villagers knew this, but since the patients were not unhappy with his treatment, he was neither acknowledged nor denounced as a Jew.

At some point when I was around seven or eight years old, I began to question my mother about the two statues in our living room—two Buddhas that had escaped the Nazi pillage. My mother explained to me that there were religions other than Catholicism. So I asked: "If I were born in Benares, I would have been Hindu; in Baghdad, Muslim; in Africa, Animist?"

I had the bad idea of sharing my questions with Madame Tocqueville, who was visibly embarrassed and had no response. That stupefied me. Could it be that faith depended on the place where one was born, on one's social group, on pure chance? Where was God in all this? All the discussions of Grace and "a special connection with Jesus" seemed weak arguments against the sheer fact of geographical determination. Without knowing it, I had just acquired the seed for innumerable religious doubts that were to last for the rest of my life.

While I was personally spared the atrocities visited on Jews, I was to learn the bitter lesson of racism. Fleury-sur-Andelle is peopled with Normands, many of whom are the descendants of Vikings. Many are red-headed with pale skin, and some still have the family name Odent, recalling the Scandinavian god Odin. My two sisters and I, with our dark skin and frizzy hair, could not pass unnoticed. Even in church, in the presence of God, the local kids couldn't resist making fun of us and calling us *les bamboulas*—a derogatory slang term for blacks.

What I did not know at the time was that racism and anti-Semitism were politically intertwined. As of September 28, 1940, a poster in the Vichy train station listed the names of certain groups who were not allowed to cross the line of demarcation between the free zone and the occupied zone: "Jews, Moroccans, Blacks, Martiniquais, Indochinese, and, as a general rule, all brown-skinned people."

Throughout the war, I was a very solitary child. For four years, I never played with any children my own age. For my mother, with her pretentions, it was unthinkable that I should play with the village kids, peasants without any manners! As for my sisters, except at meals, I scarcely saw them. In the morning, I was at school with Madame Tocqueville. In the afternoon, my sisters and I changed roles; they replaced me at school, and I, in turn, did my homework.

Fortunately, the arts provided a magical refuge. First, music. Two or three times a week, my mother opened an enormous upright piano, which had been the companion of her travels overseas. I adored listening to my mother play: she was devoted to Beethoven, Chopin, and Rachmaninov, as well as musicians less known to the French, such as Brahms. On the radio, we listened only to classical music and knew nothing of popular music or something called "jazz."

Most of all, I became a compulsive reader. My mother salvaged from our first house about twenty books of history and biography, the mutilated remains of the family library. I also discovered poetry. I was seven or eight when I learned the rules of rhyme, and this passionate apprenticeship prepared me for a lifelong devotion to reading and writing poetry.

And I learned to draw. I was four years old when my father put crayons in my hands and showed me how to use them by drawing alongside me. Years later at Fleury, during the war, I would draw for hours and hours at a stretch.

For Christmas 1942 and 1943, my mother and grandparents did their best to spoil us, but toys were rare and expensive. I have retained one marvelous memory: a Christmas tree shining with tiny candles and silver balls. Even a few presents provided great pleasure, since they were new! At the first or second Christmas, each of my sisters received a doll and I a small model of an armor-plated Cardinal Richelieu. Naturally, we felt very spoiled.

There was only one negative point. In one of my childhood books I had read that poor children put a shoe in front of the fireplace on Christmas eve, and that on Christmas day they find an orange inside it. So, I exclaimed, "We are so poor that we don't even get an orange!"

In spite of these special occasions, for four years we were subject to hunger, cold, and the fear of bombs. Food was the primary cause of our anxiety. My father had died prematurely, so his retirement pay was not very large. Moreover, the farmers in our area systematically took advantage of food shortages so as to profit from the black market.

To acquire any little thing, we had to stand in line at the grocery store, at the butcher shop, at the dairy. Several times a week, we'd spend forty-five minutes in the freezing cold before even entering a shop, and only then find out there was nothing left for sale. But one time, when accompanying my mother, I discovered a clandestine practice. I watched as the shopkeeper looked to the right, then the left, and then drew out from under the counter a bit of the desired item, that was offered to the customer at an elevated price. Then more glances around to make sure the practice remained secret.

Butter sold at the price of gold. Commercial milk was neither pasteurized nor low-fat, and one would extract the cream very carefully. Every Saturday morning, I would offer to turn the milk because I knew that I could slip a furtive finger inside when the liquid entered the exquisite phase of whipped cream. Ahha! Memory still holds the taste.

Ultimately, a little lump of butter would be formed. It was precious because it had to last the whole week. The very next day, on Sunday, the maid asked a ritual question: "Madame, can I scrape a little butter on the children's biscuits?" Scrape? That was the correct word.

Everyone in the village kept at least one hen for eggs. Rabbits were even easier to raise. My sisters and I liked to see these little creatures move around in their hutches. We would go to pick grass for them from the country paths. When the time came to turn them into food, my grandfather killed them in secret.

Grandfather was our savior. To assure that we had enough to eat, he worked hard in both his garden and ours. I had no idea of the effort required to grow the smallest vegetable. He spent hours watering, pruning, cutting, and pulling up weeds. In my own small plot, he taught me to grow carrots, peas, green beans, and lettuce. It gave me great pride to see my family eventually consume my little produce. When the potato leaves appeared, it was urgent to fight the beetles. A bit of copper sulfate would have sufficed, but it was impossible to find during the war, so my sisters and I, with little jars in our hands, slipped between the rows of plants and, from leaf after leaf, pushed the insects and larva into the jars. Then this repugnant harvest was thrown into the fire.

One has to experience the brutal winters in Normandy to know how much suffering the cold can cause. After living under the burning sun of Djibouti, we were all the more sensitive to the cold. The kitchen was the best heated room in the house, warmed by an enormous black solid-fuel stove. When our supply of wood ran low, grandfather found a way—by exchanging fruit and vegetables—to procure enough to keep the stove burning. Every evening, we undressed in the kitchen. Upstairs, where the rooms were freezing, we slept under enormous quilts. The maid put an old-fashioned warming pan between the sheets.

Doing laundry was a spectacle that my sisters and I never missed. The women of the village, many of them quite old, pushed heavy wheelbarrows carrying enormous packages to the municipal washhouse at the edge of the Andelle River. There, each one would kneel on a little three-sided slab that was opened at the back to the water, and spend hours beating the laundry by hand. Their only pleasure was gossiping. At the washhouse they exchanged all the village tittle-tattle.

To escape the worst part of the drudgery, our maid, Hélène, boiled the laundry in an enormous cauldron placed in a lean-to outside the house. When soap was scarce and costly, she replaced it with burnt wood ash that acted as a type of bleach. To dry the laundry in the sun and wind, Hélène stretched the sheets out on a rope strung up between two posts in the back of the yard. Then she pinned up the remaining items. My sisters and I never missed this spectacle. We always offered our help, which was so messy and ineffective that Hélène refused every time.

In 1944, as the Allies were preparing for their landing in Normandy, they bombarded strategic German defense points. The Americans took maximum precautions: their squadrons flew at 10,000 meters, as far as possible from German anti-aircraft guns. The English flew much lower; you could recognize them right away by a sharp whistling sound when they swooped down upon their targets.

But we'd long grown accustomed to bombing raids, which had begun in 1940. Rouen, the big city nearby, had been slowly destroyed by firebombs, usually dropped at night. The Americans dropped their bombs from so high up that they rarely hit their intended targets—the large bridges over the Seine or the train station—but they demolished almost everything nearby.

The fires were so great that even in Fleury the nocturnal sky glowed red toward Rouen.

Our village was wrapped in mourning after a young Fleury bride traveling to Rouen perished three weeks after her marriage and was buried in her wedding gown. In spite of our fears, our mother was obliged to go to Rouen to take one of my sisters to the dentist and to consult an optician for me. This man, something of a scoundrel, persuaded us that I was destined to become blind, but that, while waiting for this fearsome blindness, I could wear a pair of very expensive glasses that he would make. At each visit to Rouen, we saw ruins, more and more ruins, especially along the Seine. Finally, nothing remained of the magnificent quays from the eighteenth century.

Part of the cathedral collapsed and the roof of its north tower burned, but luckily the four pillars holding up an immense bronze spire held firm. A less fortunate fate was in store for the Palace of Justice, the largest civic building in France, dating from the Middle Ages. It was reduced to ruins. On a personal level, we knew a jeweler who had a store close to the cathedral. On one of our visits, we discovered a gaping hole in place of his jewelry store. Subsequently, we were happy to find out that he was on the other bank of the river when his shop was destroyed.

For a long time, Fleury-sur-Andelle was spared. We watched with fascination, but without fear, the flights going over our heads toward Rouen, Le Havre, or Evreux. German anti-aircraft defenses fired against them without stop, and sometimes reached their target. Whenever a plane was hit, it separated itself from the others, burst into flame, and zigzagged to the ground, sending up black smoke. And there were also white objects that descended from the sky: parachutes. Aviators jumped into the void, even with the risk of being captured once they had reached the ground. One afternoon, a plane looked enormous as it flew so close it skimmed the roofs, then passed our village. Flaming and smoking, it crashed into the fields. It seemed clear that the pilot had wanted to save us, and to make sure he could fly far enough away, he didn't pull his escape cord. He had chosen to sacrifice himself.

One day when I was at school around ten o'clock, I heard the roar of airplanes coming closer, then a terrifying noise: the bombardment of Fleury had begun. Madame Tocqueville told us to recite prayers. For my part, I looked at the table at the back of the room and wanted to slip under it. During a short period of calm, Hélène came to fetch me. Then then the bombing began again.

My mother, my sisters, Hélène, and I took refuge in the garage at the back of our garden. Its concrete roof was too thin to protect us from any strike. But for want of anything better, we stayed there for an interminable quarter hour, within a deafening din, huddled together, asking ourselves every minute if the next bomb would be for us. When the thunder stopped, we hesitated: was it safe to leave the shelter? We waited. Then a third wave began. Finally, there was a longer period of calm, and we dared return to the house. Two of our three cats joined us. One of them had been injured and was limping.

Fear took hold. We expected another alert at any time. At church, from time to time during mass, one could hear stained glass fall to the floor. I was afraid because the organ gave off the same sound as the airplane motors. I thought I was hearing the arrival of air squadrons.

Most villagers assumed the national highway was the obvious target of the bombing. My grandfather, worried that our house was too close to the highway, urged us to move to his. Having acquired experience in the trenches of World War I, he dug a kind of underground cellar in his garden, covered by two meters of dirt packed down on logs. My sisters and I hated to go down into it, where we had to squeeze together in a dark hole. And we rejoiced when, after two or three months, the rain weakened the walls and the shelter fell apart. Then we had to shelter in the cellar in his house, which he had considered inadequate earlier.

Our grandparents' house was close to the train station, another likely target for destruction, so we eventually decided to return to our own house. Shortly after our return, the Germans requisitioned two rooms: my mother received an order to lodge an officer and his orderly. Things didn't go too badly because, to their surprise, the two men could speak to my mother in their own language. It was clear that they were weary and fairly discouraged, and no longer believed in a German victory.

The orderly was a professional musician. He would look at the piano, but didn't dare touch it. But trying to find acceptable subjects of conversation, he liked to evoke the names of his favorite composers. When my mother asked him what he planned to do after the war, he boasted: "When we have won the war, I shall direct a large orchestra." My mother dared suggest otherwise: "And if you lose?" He sighed: "I shall have a very little orchestra."

The German troops benefited from occupation laws that imposed a priority system for all their needs. They lacked for nothing. We watched with surprise and envy when the orderly brought in baskets filled with meat, vegetables, fruits. . . . So much food! As he prepared the food on our stove top, my mother watched him work and said: "Aren't you ashamed to fry eggs in front of three children who are dying of hunger!" The two soldiers then shared some of their food with us.

Around the time of the Normandy landing, the Germans left our town, without exacting reprisals: we were spared the atrocities that occurred elsewhere, as in Oradour-sur-Glane.

Then one morning, a rumor started to spread: "There they are! There they are! The Americans have come!" All along the road, villagers lined up in front of their doors. In the distance, we could see a line of vehicles arriving from the direction of Rouen. They approached. Then there they were in front of us! Tanks, enormous tanks! I had probably seen some earlier, and certainly the newspapers had shown photos of German tanks. But now, with my eyes wide open, I felt I was seeing such stupefying machines for the first time. These were the real ones, they moved! On their caterpillar tracks, they moved noisily. An incredible spectacle!

The tank tops rose and smiling heads emerged, then men up to their waists. They drew women toward them with their outstretched arms, women who climbed up to kiss them.

Applause! Everyone was crying for joy! Emotions were at their peak! The men in the tanks threw out tiny objects, one of which hit my forehead. Intrigued, I discovered something totally new, the use of which I couldn't figure out at all: chewing gum.

The tanks passed and disappeared. Even at the end of the day, the excitement hadn't died down. We went to sleep very late, our heads filled with unforgettable visions.

Such a glorious day—at best, we're lucky to have one like that every century.

It's not surprising that the war left me with very bad memories. For many years, painful episodes erupted into my nightmares, where I relived the anguish of bombardment. The sight and sound of airplanes continued to fill me with fear. As children, we don't have a real sense of danger. My sisters and I wanted TO SEE. Often, around midnight, we would sneak out to watch airplanes drop their rockets and light up the sky. It was a captivating spectacle. Now, so many years later, when lightning streaks across the sky, I say: "I adore storms. Their bursts of light don't drop bombs."

Having experienced intense hunger as a child, I never enter a grocery store now without marveling: "To think that I can buy as much as I like!" Even now pastry shop windows dazzle me. Also, to this day, I am incapable of forgetting the cold in Normandy, nor can I express how much I appreciate contemporary methods of heating.

However, as I quickly became aware, my experience was awful, but no more than that. At the end of 1944, we discovered the horror of the Holocaust. We had to confront unbearable and appalling photos—the sight of a hundred mass graves, of stacks of cadavers piled up in death camps. The terror caused by these images made me realize how comparatively little I had suffered, and what luck I had had.

Because of the war, my orphan childhood was painful and sad, but there had been so much worse.

# CHAPTER FOUR

# Within the War Machine

*A Nazi Childhood*

*Winfried Weiss* was born and raised in Franconia, Germany, where he spent the war years. His father was an officer in the Ordnungspolizei, the gendarmerie, which was the uniformed police force throughout Germany. The members of the Ordnungspolizei, which was controlled by the SS, wore green uniforms, and were known colloquially as the "green police." Winfried often refers to his father and his colleagues as the green, or apple, gendarmes.

His memoir, *A Nazi Childhood*, was published in 1983. It reveals a side of the war very different from the other accounts in this book, and is remarkable for its distinct values and perspective. Yet it also shows the many similarities between his childhood experience in Nazi Germany and the experiences of children in countries on the Allied side, beginning, in the excerpt presented here, with an abrupt change in living arrangements, as Winfried and his family—his mother and father, and his sisters Ilse and Gertrude—move from the idyllic rural setting of Pfarrweisach to the more urban Kitzingen.

FRANCE HAD SURRENDERED—our *Telefunken* (radio) said so. Summer 1940. We went on long walks every Sunday afternoon, my mother in an organdy dress, my father in suit and tie with the party button on his lapel, my sisters in light summer dresses. During one of our outings, my father shot the most successful childhood picture of me. It was blown up and my mother put it on her night table.

I'm standing in a field of grass and clover. Some of the plants are so high they reach to my shoulders. At my back are two apple trees, slightly out of focus. My knees show round and pudgy in my short pants, held up by white suspenders with edelweiss embroidered on them. My pants have an embroidered flap up front, easy to unbutton whenever I had to take a leak. Someone had put the SS insignia on the flap. Sharp and angular, the emblem looks like two flashing thunderbolts. All is innocence and sun. Cirrus-blue summer clouds move above, and I am smiling radiantly into the camera holding a daisy. One is tempted to kiss my healthy cheeks, grown fat on Franconian milk and sausages.

In October 1940, just when Hitler decided to postpone the invasion of England, my father was promoted to Meister of the Gendarmerie. We received another heavy piece of parchment signed by the president of the German Gendarmerie and by Hitler (in proxy of course) under an eagle with a swastika, saying that my father had been promoted in the name of the Führer and Volk, and that we had been transferred to Kitzingen.

After Pfarrweisach, Kitzingen was immense. My sister Gertrude took me up to the attic and showed me the sights. She wagged her index finger at me and pointed in different directions. I followed her finger across the red tile roofs of Kitzingen dotted with church spires. There was a river called Main that divided the town from a suburb called Etwashausen, meaning something sticking out. Vineyards grew along the river, and Kitzingen had industry. There was an airfield in the east and large barracks to the west. And it would take us much longer now to reach "*die Natur*" for our Sunday walks.

Nineteen forty-one was a big year for Germany. We swept through North Africa. Our *Telefunken* reported one big news event after another. While the tubes glowed with an orange light and the cat's eye quivered when we had static, the loudspeaker announced that President Roosevelt had signed the Lend-Lease Act [authorizing the U.S. to provide weapons to Great Britain and its allies]; but Germany was able to cope with it.

Hitler and Göring hung on the east wall of our big entrance hall with the gothic arches—two color photographs framed and under glass. A crest of laurels with the words "Gendarmerie Kitzingen" hung between them. Every time I left the house or entered, Hitler and Göring were in their proper places surrounded by the smell of waxed floors and humid, whitewashed walls. Both wore brown uniforms with capes flung backwards. A leather strap ran across Hitler's chest. Göring had his left hand resting against his hip. Hitler his right. Göring had a marshal's baton in his right hand. "Like a fat little emperor," a friend of my mother said as they came down the staircase. "Shhh!" my mother said, putting her index finger across her lips.

Jews were ghosts. I had never seen any, but they existed because people talked about them. The word *"Jude"* came out of their mouths unlike other words. It wasn't a neutral word. People said *"Jude," "Jüdin,"* or *"Juden,"* with a particular tone in their voices. They charged the words with colors that they didn't give other words. "Jew" always insinuated things; it produced undulating waves of hidden emotions. When people told stories about Jews, my ear picked up on the unsaid things: repulsive, dark, dirty, dangerous, funny, mocking, comical, alien, and sad.

Pfarrweisach didn't have any Jews. But Kitzingen had a Jewish history, especially around the Landwehrplatz. At the north end of the linden trees was the shell of a big synagogue with two towers. It was boarded up. It had burned during the *Kristallnacht*, while I, cuddled in warm blankets in my bed in Pfarrweisach, had peacefully slept into my first birthday.

And across from the old monastery where we lived was an abandoned red building with gothic windows that looked like blind eyes onto the Landwehrstrasse. My parents told me that they didn't know what it was, but a neighbor said it was a Jewish school; it had been closed a few years back. "You should have heard the noise they made in there," she said. She started to imitate the noise: she clucked like a hen and revolved her tongue in her open mouth. It sounded as if she had an apple in her mouth while unfamiliar sounds rose and fell: Jewish children learning Hebrew, an alien language. "*Hebraisch*" sounded in the neighbor's mouth like something that should be flushed down the toilet.

Before my eyes Jews and Jewesses crystalized: ghosts made up of the same qualities that people had in the tone of their voices and attached to the characters in their stories.

Tanta Anna said that one of the Jewesses living across the road from her always took some work with her when she went into the outhouse. She even would take a bowl of dough with her. She kneaded the dough into submission. Pale dough reminded me of unwashed hands. Jews had pale, unwashed hands. Jews were connected with toilets, urination, and defecation. And then one day, while I pretended I was playing in a corner while the adults spoke to each other in low voices, I heard them say that the German army in Czechoslovakia had captured a nest of Jews who had kidnapped and killed little Christian boys and girls and used their blood in baking matzos. They said they had found the small carcasses in a kosher butcher shop hanging from hooks like pigs and cows. I was a little Christian boy.

To the color of defiled, pale dough came the burst of blood and terror. Jews and Jewesses smelling like garlic chased little boys down the road. I was one of them. I was terrified and fascinated. Sometimes I was captured. My imagination stopped in a white butcher's shop with gleaming hooks, like the shop where my mother bought her meat. Dark bearded and hairy men with big noses overpowered me. Jews.

While Germany invaded Russia and while Churchill and Roosevelt met on the Atlantic, my mind assembled from various elements what my ears had extracted from the adults' conversations—lurid scenes of terror over and over again. I was always on the verge of being captured by dark hairy Jews who wanted to hang me from a hook. The external work went on as usual. Nobody suspected that I was pursued by imaginary Jews.

Once in a while I visited my father in the office; he took me on his knees and let me type. He smelled like cigarette smoke. Over his desk was another photograph of Hitler, sepia-colored, his hair slicked down. Behind me in a cupboard were nightsticks, guns, and revolvers. The other gendarmes patted me on the head and said, *"Na, wie geht's Winfried?"* [How goes it, Winfried?]. When Lieutenant Nüsslein came in, I stood up and shook hands with him, making a deep bow, a *"Diener."* *"Mach'n schönen Diener"* [Make a deep bow], my mother always told me, because the lieutenant was above us in rank. His wife gave me a chocolate once in a while. I made bows clear down to the floor, and she always exclaimed, "What a polite little boy!"

Germany was at the peak of her power. The gendarmes had a big map of Europe and Africa on the wall; they had used red ink to shade in the territories that Germany held. The whole world was shaded red.

Our *Telefunken* announced Pearl Harbor a day after St. Nicholas had brought me apples and candy in his large bag. *"Ach Gott!"* my mother said to neighbors. "Where will it all end?" But everybody said that one or two more enemies wouldn't matter; the Americans had a bad army and they were all cowards. In the gendarmerie everything went on as usual. . . .

The German Army opened its summer offensive in Russia; all went well. The *Telefunken* glowed during the evening, and Gertrude said that this time we were going to get old Stalin, we were bombing Moscow. The linden blossoms were drying in linen bags in the pantry. Every time someone opened the door the kitchen was flooded with their scent.

Lieutenant Nüsslein got into the black DKW of the gendarmerie and drove off one day. He had taken me a few times for a ride in the car. It was made completely of plastic and plywood and smelled of gasoline, stale cigarette smoke, and rubber. Lieutenant Nüsslein didn't come back. They found his car parked on a lonely country road close to Repperndorf; he had died of a heart attack.

Frau Nüsslein, who was called Frau Lieutenant Nüsslein, had red eyes; we gave our condolences. We shook hands, I bowed. Frau Nüsslein gave me a chocolate bar. On the wrapper was a turbaned Moor carrying a bowl of fruit. Frau Nüsslein cried. I smelled the chocolate through the foil. I was afraid to eat it for several days because I thought some of Lieutenant Nüsslein's death had gone into it.

Herr Nüsslein was dead; his wife moved to Hitler Strasse under the big old chestnut trees next to the railway station. The chocolate bar she had given me was the last chocolate I would see for years! After the Nüssleins left, we moved upstairs into a large apartment in the converted attic. The huge roof of the old monastery wrapped itself around us like a warm and comfortable monk's skirt. We had regular-sized rooms now and distributed the three plants we had brought from Pfarrweisach: the jade plant went into the corridor, the zimmerlinde in the living room, and the asparagus plant into the dining room. Gertrude watered them and carried them downstairs once in a while to let them have some sun. She talked to them like little cats, "There, there," she said, "get lots of sun, it's good for you," and she blew off the dust that had collected on the leaves.

Our neighbors across the hall were Lieutenant Kluge and his wife. He was in the army and always away—first on the western front and then in hospitals because he had a *bauchschuss*. A bullet had gone through his stomach and out again. Whenever I heard the word *bauchschuss*, with a strong accent on the first and second syllables, I saw a bullet (it was a French bullet, my mother had told me) go through a stomach, making a sound like the word *schuss*, snakelike, hissing, tearing into matter that looked like the stomach of a rabbit or pig, because I had seen their stomachs. My mother spoke of Lieutenant Kluge's *bauchschuss* with a lowered voice and a solemn tone. Bauchschuss was just at the edge of death. It gave Frau Kluge a dramatic halo. I was afraid to look her straight in the eyes: a wife of a man with *bauchschuss* inspired awe.

The German Africa Corps was stopped at El Alamein. Our *Telefunken* spit out that name every night. Gertrude said that it was only temporary; we were getting our breath back before we took Egypt. We measured with a string the distance between El Alamein and Cairo. "It's nothing," Gertrude said. "We have fast tanks."

Meanwhile, in the gendarmerie, I lived a happy life. Every evening after dinner my father rocked me on his knees. He had taken off his uniform jacket and sat there with his long-sleeved underwear and suspenders. We played "*Hoppe Hoppe Reiter, wenn er fällt dann schreit er*" [Hop, hop, rider, if he falls, he will cry]. He was the horse, I was the rider. At some point, he would open his thighs and I fell through. Though he always caught me at the last moment, I had the sensation of falling into an abyss. My stomach fluttered and soon as he caught me I begged him to start all over again. I abandoned myself to the game. I bent my head backwards and shrieked with joy. I couldn't wait for my father's knees to open. According to the rhyme that went with the game, I fell into a ditch where I was eaten by ravens. His head bent toward me as I fell and he laughed as he pulled me back up onto his knees. Nothing could happen to me. My father was a green gendarme in the center of the German Reich. He made the law and I was his son. My father saved me from the black ravens. He had strong thighs, he had a hairy chest; he took care of me and my mother, as well. I slept next to them in their bedroom and could hear them breathe when I woke up in the middle of the night. Their breathing sounded warm and secure and I went back to sleep.

Gendarmes were all around me. They smelled of gasoline, leather, and tobacco. Their black boots creaked They waved at me every time they passed. One of them lived in a small room for unmarried gendarmes. Sometimes he came to us in the evening. When he saw me, he clicked his heels and said, "Heil Hitler!" Everybody laughed and I blushed.

My mother was on her knees. It was her turn to wax the staircase. She was talking to Frau Lieutenant Kluge: the two women didn't see me come into the entrance hall where Hitler and Göring demanded a perfectly polished gendarmerie. I heard my mother say, "Did you hear him scream yesterday?" After a short pause, Frau Kluge's "Yes" floated down the hallway like a leaf that had just left the tree, unsure and fluttery. My mother's voice was more involved than Frau Kluge's; she seemed reserved, my mother emotional. My mother said, "Why do they have to beat them that hard?" When I asked her about it, my mother said nobody was beaten.

The oleanders in the pots were blooming. The typewriters were chattering in the office, and I helped Mr. Beyer to water his flowers. The apple gendarme was laughing above us, and I could hear the voice of my father and others. Franconian clouds sailed by in the summer blue.

Mr. Beyer and I listened in the direction of the open office window. Someone whimpered, then screamed and I heard the noise of shuffling chairs. A man yelled "Nein!" and then thuds, like the sound of my mother's rug beater when she hit the rug, only softer and muffled, came from the window. A man screaming again. I had never heard adults scream like that. It was shocking and embarrassing, because it was uncontrolled. The sounds were not connected with something I could see, but as part of some momentous drama. And while it went on, sparrows twittered in Herr Beyer's garden, snails drowned slowly in the bucket, the nasturtiums were dripping with water, and Frau Beyer had hung up laundry to dry in the sun. Screams from the office passed like a cold breeze over Frau Beyer's sheets.

Nothing happened. Herr Beyer laughed and said there they go again, beating someone's ass because he didn't tell the truth.

I entered a new phase that summer. Lieutenant Röhmer, who had moved into the Nüsslein's apartment, had two children. One was Wolfram, a teenager in the Hitler Jugend, and the other was Irmtraud, my age.

Everyone said that Irmtraud and I were made for each other. We were a cute couple. We were the same height, the same age, had almost the same hair-color though hers was blonder than mine. We played together all the time. I invited Irmtraud into my tree house, the old wardrobe suspended in our pear tree with the tough wormy pears.

Irmtraud introduced me to dolls. Her neatly made bed was full of dolls of all sizes. Some closed and opened their eyes, some said "Mama," others were stiff and lifeless. The minute I saw them I wanted to play with them. I was willing to leave my wind-up cars behind and put bottles into the dolls' mouths and change their diapers. There was no doubt in my mind that was what I wanted to do. But everyone said dolls weren't for boys, and so I reluctantly left them on Irmtraud's bed.

The whole neighborhood pointed to us and said we were the cutest things in Kitzingen. There is a whole series of snapshots from my Irmtraud years that show us before every possible backdrop. While Hitler played Barbarossa in Russia, we played cute in front of the neighborhood Agfas—next to the lilac bushes, in front of pansies, in our garden, in the Beyers' garden, out on the street; Irmtraud with white ribbons in her hair, we both in Sunday clothes; overexposed, underexposed, out of focus, with legs, without legs, uncentered, smiling and sullen—we survive into eternity. Two Aryan kids were growing up in an abandoned monastery, surrounded by the smell of wax and polish. We have fat and happy faces.

Irmtraud and I were in our tree house between heaven and earth, puffy clouds coasting by overhead. We were having lunch. Irmtraud had fixed salad leaves, which she served on her little dishes. While she cleaned the kitchen, I pretended I was a gendarme sitting at his desk waiting for the phone to ring. Or, it was tea time. We drank artificial lemonade and pretended it was tea. We had black war cookies with it. And while having tea one day, it happened again. A man screamed in the office above us. The windows were open, blue smoke was curling above us as usual. We heard muffled thuds. Irmtraud said, "He's getting his ass beaten." The word "*Arsch*" sounded improper in her mouth. It shocked me. She said that her daddy had told her it happened sometimes. Then Irmtraud shouted in the direction of her mother's living room that someone was being beaten in the office. My father appeared at the office window and looked down on us. The screaming stopped and he closed the window.

A beautiful spring morning in 1942, sunny and brilliant. It is in the nature of things that the Jews should leave on the noon train. It has happened that my father, the gendarme, will be in charge of the entire operation. Over a cup of barley coffee at the kitchen table, he says to my mother: "It's not fair to ask us to do it! It's not our responsibility!" My mother nods her head in silent agreement.

When I come downstairs the Judenschule is surrounded by the police. The red building seems alive, full of unseen creatures. Sometimes a shadow appears at a window, but is quickly drawn back inside.

I ask my mother about this. She is at the stove. She turns down the flame and without looking once at me says carefully, Oh, they are Jewish people, they were moved in during the night—they're not staying long, they're leaving on the noon train.

My mother then says, go play in the garden today, your father doesn't want you out in the street.

But I don't listen: I go stand at the corner of our house in the shade, so my father—my beloved gun-belted, uniformed hero—cannot see me.

My father, the other gendarmes and the city police are milling around in front of the school. Over them, a tall, thin, white-haired old man wearing a pince-nez stands at one of the upper windows. He shakes his fist at the street below, then suddenly two arms pull him back. But the old man reappears: he pops up again like a puppet in a Punch-and-Judy show, jerky and violent. The old man shouts: *I refuse . . . you scum.* He uses the word *Abschaum*, an old-fashioned and solemn word. Then again, two ghostly arms pull him back inside.

Below, the gendarmes and the police are chattering with each other, laughing as always. It seems like a holiday, a *kermesse*, animated, full of life. It is the old man in the window who is out of place in the ordinariness of life on the Landwehrstrasse.

But my father is acting strange. His behavior keeps me well back in the shadows. He makes me feel guilty, watching him. He stands motionless in his green uniform in front of the open doors of the Judenschule and stares at the pavement with such intensity that I expect him to receive a message at any moment from the silent ground.

Again, the old man appears at the window. His behavior, too, is strange and embarrassing to me. When he shouts the same words again—*You scum!*—one of the gendarmes pulls out his gun and, laughing, points it at the window. My father looks up, then orders the officer to put the gun away.

Suddenly from one of the upper windows of the Jewish school a large case flies out and into the street. It breaks open and silver forks and spoons scatter over the Landwehrstrasse. The gendarmes duck. A china coffee pot follows. It lands not far from me against the yellow walls of our gendarmerie. This pot has a flower pattern. It bursts into hundreds of pieces against the wall, but the spout stays intact and rolls toward me. It is graceful, shaped like a slender torso, shiny, new, with traces of the flower pattern, ready to pour coffee at any moment. I retreat from the shiny object and hide in the shadows. One of the policemen bends and gathers up the silver spoons and forks and put them back into the case. He even breathes against the silver and polishes it on his sleeves, taking a long time doing it, then carefully tucks the case on the ledge of one of the lower windows of the Beyer house.

Somebody is emptying a briefcase of paper into the street from the upper floor of the Judenschule, little pieces fall in excited patterns and scatter over the juniper bushes. A voice shouts down from the same window, "You won't get anything from me! I'd rather destroy it than let you get your dirty paws on it!"

Other hands throw out more shredded papers. My father has his back to the building and doesn't notice this snowstorm. As I watch, little white balls fragment into tiny pieces that float silently to the ground. Boxes now begin to sail out of the windows . . . and as if that were the cue, a policeman plunges inside; I can hear him shout, OUT! EVERYBODY OUT!

One of the gendarmes is striking the iron grills on the ground floor windows with his nightstick. It makes a deep echo inside the school. The sound is effective. Invisible creatures from the inside are streaming out as if the sound of the nightstick is too much for their ears. Men, women, children: the old man with the pince-nez is there too; he's on the arm of a young girl, muttering to himself. Everyone is carrying a small suitcase, even the children. A thin old woman appears. She has a long, skinny nose like the beak of a bird; her glasses have slid far down. She is wearing a brown coat and a brown hat with flowers on it. She steps right up to my father and shouts: "You can't do this!" "*Ich gehe nicht! Hören Sie? Ich gehe nicht!*" "I won't go! Do you hear me? I won't!" She pushes her face right into my father's. He looks straight past her, he says nothing. The apple gendarme takes hold of the old woman's arm and leads her back into the column of people.

The column marches up the Würzburger Strasse until it reaches the Falterturm, where it turns left. I am following, hidden in the shadows of the bushes along the avenue. We leave the gas works behind and turn into the Adolf Hitler Strasse, which leads to the train station. Suddenly, the thin old woman steps out of the column and begins to shout. She shakes her fist at the gendarmes, then at my father, who doesn't see her. The gendarme laughs, grabs her arm, pats her on the back: "*Du alte Giftnudel, du*" . . . "You poisonous old noodle, can't you be quiet?" But the woman stubbornly sets her suitcase on the ground. Her voice is high and shrill, it rises above all the noise on the street. The column begins to fall apart. The old woman has her arms high in the air and is waving them back and forth; her mouth forms shrieking words I do not understand. Near her is a little boy about my age carrying a small suitcase. He is wearing long brown stockings under his short pants; I am wearing the same. One of the gendarmes penetrates the column and gives the old woman a gentle shove; he says, "Will you get on now, you crazy old woman?" The column slowly begins to move again beneath the towering chestnut trees. In the gardens in front of the old houses along the Adolf Hitler Strasse the hawthorn trees are in bloom, exploding with color.

At the end of the wide avenue I can see the station. I stop and watch from behind the grill of the freight yard. A train stands belching black smoke on platform three, its old third-class carriages with no connecting platforms, the kind of train we take to Würzburg. The gendarmes motion the people from the Judenschule to various carriages. The ancient locomotive gathers speed. I run home as fast as I can.

My father never knows that I watched him that bright morning.

Sometime during 1942 my father decided to become an officer. While Irmtraud and I played gendarme and wife in the pear tree, my parents felt that an officer would offer greater advantages to his family. He went for officers' training in Freiburg, in the Black Forest. My father finished with C's in all his courses, three points above the class average. He got a large certificate, with eagles, swastikas, and signatures by commanders and the Führer. It was signed and stamped on December 18, 1942.

It was Spring 1943. As usual the chestnuts bloomed. I played with Irmtraud in the pear tree; she served tea, she was my wife; we spanked our child, her big doll, because Irmtraud said our child didn't want to play the piano.

My father came back from Freiburg in his black boots and green uniform. He was my familiar father. He hadn't changed. The shape and scent of his body (cigarettes and a faint smell of sweat) embraced me constantly, and I clung to them unconsciously for protection. It never occurred to me that it could end, that my father's green uniform could walk out of the gendarmerie and never return. I wasn't aware that the blue smoke of his Russian cigarettes wouldn't always curl out of the office window behind the vines; that his presence, his gestures and motions were limited in time, that my father was about to pass from my view into territories where he couldn't take me.

One day in July, while Irmtraud and I sat in our pear tree, an officer rang our bell. Since my father was out getting a haircut there is no record of how he would have confronted the news. But my mother cried at once when the officer told her, that since he was a personal friend of my father, he wanted to tell him himself that my father had been ordered to go to Russia in August. Russia! My mother cried, Russia was doom and destruction! *Russland*! She repeated that my father had chronic bronchitis, and that he had been already at the front in the first war. The Russian winter would be the worst thing for his bronchitis.

I had come down from the pear tree and listened to the adults in the living room that was reserved for Christmas and special occasions. The SS-officer nodded his head sympathetically when my mother said this wasn't fair, they couldn't do this to us. The officer shrugged his shoulders apologetically; my mother offered him a glass of schnapps and he lit a cigarette. He shook my hand and patted my head. "You will have to look after your mother now," he said. "You'll be the man in the house!"

August 1, 1943. In a daring long-range attack, the Americans bombed the oil fields of Ploesti (in Romania) to destroy our resources. We walked my father to the station as if we were out on a Sunday stroll, as if nothing was happening. Up the Landwehrstrasse, through the square arch of the Neue Brücke, up the hill along the old chestnut trees of the Adolf Hitler Strasse that lead right into the railway station. We are out on the platform with him. It is a sunny day; my mother quietly cries and dabs her eyes. "Don't worry," my father is saying. "I'll be back in three months, it's promised!" To me he says be a good student this fall. The train arrives on platform number three. My father gets into a second class compartment and comes back out to embrace us once more; the conductor shoves him gently back in. The train moves out in the direction of Nürnberg, East, in big puffs of smoke. Slow at first, it moves faster and faster until my father who is leaning out of the window and waving a white handkerchief is so small that my eyes can no longer make him out. And, thus my father, his gendarme-green aura in black boots, disappeared forever from my life.

Somewhere in the dark night of November 28/29, my father and his Ukrainians were ambushed by Russian guerrillas three kilometers west of Vladyslawczik. Silence falls forever. My father, the uncoded cipher sinks into the snows of Russia. The rest: kind letters from commanding officers, comrades, testimonials, my father's picture surrounded by laurels and the SS-insignia, in-the-name-of-the-Führer.

Nobody was present when life went out of him, no witnesses. He disappeared forever while I lay cuddled in my warm Franconian bed.

Saint Michael was my father's patron saint. He had wings, a flaming sword and shield, and slew dragons. My father had a green motorcycle, black boots, and gendarme's gun. He was the archangel who killed my dragons until the dark slew him.

By the fall of 1943, the dragons entered my territory from all directions. There were the monsters of the night: Lancasters, Wellingtons, Stirlings, Handley-Page Halifaxes that had been waiting for my father's departure. They flew deeper and deeper into the German Reich. We tried to ignore them but as the horror stories increased, we ran every time the sirens wailed. At night, they made my teeth chatter.

Nights, when I was deep in comfortable sleep, the sirens rose to a high-pitched wail that rattled the windows. The sound penetrated my ears, shot down my spinal column and exited through my toes. I dressed quickly in the cold room. Enemy planes on the chart over my bed were out there in the air. Olive green Lancasters with incendiary bombs. My bed looked warm and white under the soft light of the lamp. The folds threw cozy shadows, but I had to walk across the night garden. I knew that English pilots hung high up there in the night with oxygen masks on their faces. Massive hulks in black spaces were approaching.

We stumbled with our gas masks and emergency suitcases, I holding on to my mother. Our dark corridor had unusual shadows. Gertrude once put on woolen underpants for a sweater. She didn't notice it until people laughed in the shelter.

The other people in the dark hall sounded hollow and unearthly. The familiar had retreated. Territory I knew so well by day wore a different face.

Only four years before, Germany had destroyed Poland, now the Germans were retreating from Russia. And I had to go to school. Aunt Augusta brought me to school: the Roman Catholic Elementary

School for Boys at the end of the Schrannenstrasse. I had Gertrude's old leather satchel strapped to my back, pre-war quality, eternal, they all said. Waxed and polished, made from Franconian cows. I had a new wooden box with a removable top. Inside: pencils and slate stylos for writing on the small slate blackboards we all possessed. A sponge in a green box to wipe the slate clean, eraser, and pencil sharpener.

We assembled in the courtyard and sang the national anthem under a limp September swastika next to the tall chestnut trees of the St. Johannis Kirche, late Renaissance. Dark green trees with sun spots coming through. We raised our hands: Heil Hitler! Then we went inside. Hard smell of oiled floors and sweating children. For me, it was an aggressive alien odor.

Frau Baumann was my first teacher. She had black braids wrapped around her head and wore the party button over her heart. She ordered the parents to the back of the room, and sorted us out according to height. The mothers didn't say a word, which made a deep impression on us. Even parents were helpless before Frau Baumann. She ruled unopposed, especially over us, the fatherless. We sat according to height. Frau Baumann had judged and ranked us already. I became aware there was a hierarchy, and I was about in the center of it.

Frau Baumann stood erect in front of us. In the corner to her left was a large cane. Behind her on the wall, Hitler: sepia-red, looking into the easterly direction. He had better things to do than to watch us.

I accepted the fact that I now lived in a world of women. They accomplished everything, although ultimate authority came from men. As more and more men went off to war, women took their places. All the women said the same thing: "*Wer hätte das gedacht.*" "Who would have thought it would come to this?" They went on to say it couldn't be helped, they had to suffer, but they expected to surrender their present roles which they had usurped from men sometime in the future, when peace would restore the old world order. I was living in a temporary world, the war-world in which old rules no longer applied. Children were to be pitied because they had to endure war. "Why did we bring children into the world?" they said shaking their heads. We were poor worms, *Würmchen*. I felt a soft glow from all the sympathy but didn't understand much else because war was all I could remember.

As 1943 declined, so did German strength. The Allies increased their activities. At a series of conferences in far-flung places that we found in my sister's atlas, they met to decide on my fate: Cairo, Casablanca, Teheran, Aunt Anna said, were the cause for my rickets! Her house had been blown up by the Americans in Schweinfurt. She brought a new game with her, inspired by the allied meetings.

In the evening, as soon as the blackout curtains were drawn, we sat around the table and played blowing-up-the-Allies. All we needed were matches and a clothespin.

Aunt Anna emptied the matches on the table, snipped off one of the match tops and stuck the explosive head in the prongs of the open clothespin. It looked like an alligator whose mouth was forcefully opened. Then she put the empty lower half of the match box on top of the clothespin, which represented a hotel in Teheran. She did all the voices herself: a knock, the hotel owner answered, and Stalin asked for a room. Stalin was a match Aunt Anna put to bed in the hotel. Then Roosevelt came and was put in the same bed. Finally Churchill. Then Hitler asked for a bed. He was invited to join the others but refused. He lit the match between the clothespin and with a hissing explosion the hotel blew sky high. Everybody applauded and Aunt Anna said she would wring Churchill's neck personally if she had the chance. He was behind everything. He was the cause of suffering and the terrible bombings. Churchill was a gangster of the worst kind, a killer of innocent children.

Neither the RAF nor the USAAF had dropped anything on Kitzingen yet, but one day the sirens went off exactly at noon. B-24s appeared out of the blue and tried to hit the railway bridge in the south of town. All the bombs missed, sounding like distant thunder. Everything was over quickly and we emerged from the Beyers' shelter. We had been warned, the enemy hadn't forgotten us.

Soon afterwards the anti-aircraft guns went off at night. From the kitchen window we watched tracer bullets flying into the sky like celestial fireworks. Instead of running to the shelter we were hypnotized by the spectacle. We heard planes overhead and suddenly colored flares floated from the skies over Kitzingen. The apple gendarme screamed from downstairs that this was it, we were going to burn tonight. The whole house ran to the shelter, the Riedels screamed and prayed. We all knew that the flares, nicknamed Christmas trees, were always dropped by lead planes to mark the target for the following bomber fleets. We sat on the pre-war orange crates and waited with pounding hearts for sound of the monster Lancasters that had killed 50,000 in Hamburg; the fire had consumed all the oxygen and people suffocated in the streets and cellars. Aunt Augusta had vividly described people in flames running through the streets and jumping into the harbor to douse the burning phosphor. My heart stopped at the faintest sound. What did the English want in Kitzingen? The RAF didn't come that night. The apple gendarme explained the bombers didn't see the flares and missed the target. The Riedels said a loud prayer before we went upstairs.

I had started to chew and suck the leather straps of my school satchel. My mother was embarrassed about it. The straps looked pockmarked and sapped by my saliva. I couldn't help it. I couldn't resist my oral craving. On the way to school, waiting to cross a street, I chewed with passion. I tried to hide it, finally I wasn't even aware that I chewed in public. The straps were always there, never diminished. Only in Frau Baumann's presence did I resist; but I could feel the straps tempting me insidiously. Firm, yet pliable, stringent in taste, the chemistry of spit and old leather had become addictive. I sucked and chewed and rolled them with my tongue. I wanted to chew out the very soul of the leather. My mother sensed there was an underlying reason for my chewing passion, but mainly treated it as a destructive streak in me that sought to destroy a perfectly good pre-war satchel impossible to replace. But I was sucking on something more profound.

I also had another habit that worried my mother. I looked like an idiot doing it, she said. I ran the fingernails of my right hand over my earlobes, particularly when they were cold. Something urged me to absorb the coolness of my earlobes with my fingers.

February 23, 1945, started out like a good day. It was warm, the air smelled like spring and buds on the linden trees were beginning to swell. I wore knee pants and white socks, and remember distinctly how warm the sun felt on my naked knees. My knees remember well.

In our dining room we still had our Christmas tree from 1944; it looked like a relic, a dry skeleton with ornaments from another time. The room had been too cold, we had no fuel, so nobody had taken it down. My mother kept saying it was a disgrace and she hoped the neighbors wouldn't see it; it wouldn't have happened if father were still here.

On the Landwehrplatz we sat in the sun; Rolfi said that the Luftwaffe had stationed new jets on our airfield. The jets were going to sweep the Americans from the skies; the Americans were cowards anyway, they had no discipline; in our apartment my mother was cooking dumplings, because she had gotten some meat that morning, it was going to be a good lunch for a change. The air seduced our souls to grow wings the only way we knew—as airplanes. Airplanes triumphed over gravity: Rolfi and I were gigantic FW Condors. Anneliese was an enemy Lancaster and Margarete Riedel an American DC-3 trying to sneak in paratroopers.

Rolfi and I bombed Kiev, our shiny wings swept upward as the bomb load was released, we circled once more; the onion domes of Kiev were burning. We became Me-109s and shot down Annaliese whose greasy pigtails wobbled in the spring air as she tried to escape us. But all enemy planes were shot down; only German planes reached safety. Her engines were on fire, her crew bailed out. Our pursuit was merciless, our mechanics had installed long-range fuel tanks, we couldn't be stopped.

I cut through the sky like a sharp blade: all speed and altitude, drunk with the sunny air. But we forgot to turn our eyes to the spaces above because we thought that we were flying higher than anybody else. At two o'clock, hundreds of silvery bodies emitting white contrails streamed toward us in the unobstructed skies.

The Americans sounded the trumpets of the Last Judgment! Archangels were humming at the gates of Kitzingen, the air parted before them like the Red Sea. The Americans had launched Operation Clarion to destroy all railway centers in Germany, and fate had already given us a day of reprieve. On February 22, 38 B-17s were sent out to attack us but couldn't find Kitzingen. Early the next morning, 452 B-17s took off from southern England. They flew at an altitude of 20,000 feet right into the German Reich. While I was writing my essay for Frau Baumann, they had crossed the Schelde River through light cumulus clouds, but Franconia was perfectly clear. The angels of destruction appeared in metallic flashes of combat wings gliding into central Germany while we pursued Margarete's pigtails.

At 11:15 a.m., while my mother's potato dumplings were expanding into light fluffy balls in softly boiling water, our sirens went off. The Russian steppes, the minarets of Tunis, and the blue waters of the Atlantic vanished like mirages and we ran to our potato cellars. The sparrows we left behind in glorious isolation. Doors slammed, a car screeched, the square grew quiet. The pre-alarm warning left the world waiting for the beating of the wings.

The external world was silent, but the interior of the houses banged with noise and confusion. The Riedels were dragging out their suitcases, Gertrude stood at the window and listened for airplanes, and my mother said that everything was *beschissen*, "shat upon," because her dumplings were going to be ruined. Potato dumplings were symbols of the ordinary world to me, now on the brink of extinction. We sensed disaster. We ran to the dining room windows, the Christmas tree dropped needles as soon as the draft hit it. We could hear distant airplanes, guns boomed in the northeast. The sirens wailed a full alert. God descended to 13,500 feet.

The explosions came in waves. Sheets of bombs, *Bombenteppiche*, "carpets of bombs," dropped from the open bomb bays of the B-17s aiming for the railway yards, but the bombs came into town. I longed for the straps of my leather satchel, but it had been left behind upstairs. I was condemned to sit in the middle of our cellar and endure the dark shaking at our doors.

At 11:55 a.m. Hitler was still hanging on the wall but Frau Riedel's braids had come loose. The B-17s had left and we stood in front of the gendarmerie. My sister Ilse came running up the alley with dusty hair. She had been at her typewriter when the military hospital across the street disappeared in dust and smoke taking chunks of park with it. "Ja, ja . . . so was, so was," she said, her hands describing pointless semicircles.

The linden square looked the same, but smoke drifted down on us and the sky was no longer blue. Flakes of ash were falling, and a fine dust hung in the air which smelled musty like wet mortar and old walls.

We had been saved.

When the second wave of B-17s and their fighter escorts arrived, parts of Kitzingen were already obscured in clouds of dust and fire. The planes released clusters of 500-pound bombs that dropped into the city making the plaster fall from our ceiling. The Americans saw our monastery as an L-shaped structure below them, the linden square as an open space with bare trees, barely visible. But they didn't see me, hidden in the chaos of the dark cellar, breathing in fear and trembling. I didn't want to die. The explosions came and went, columns of dust rose into the Franconian sky. Bombs fell into the cemetery where white angels lost arms and legs, and they sent coffins into the spring air. Corpses sailed across the sun, rotting flesh and globs of decomposition stuck to the walls of neighboring houses. The church built by Petrini was hit; they got the Deuster castle and the shelters where Gertrude's schoolmates had sought safety, and, most of all, the B-17s got Frau Baumann and her clock. One of the planes unleashed the braids which had sat on her head like a crown of thorns. Frau Baumann ended in a direct hit close to the railway station, the worst place to be. Somebody afterward told us that she had been pulverized. The Americans ended Frau Baumann, my first teacher, and took over my education.

Kitzingen was already covered in dust clouds, but the third wave dropped their bombs right into that dust and smoke. The Americans had the power of life or death. They answered our prayers with fire and explosion. The potato sack in front of the cellar window swayed in the agitated air. The partitions rattled, Mahlchen moaned, and I had dust between my teeth. Our eyelashes and our hair were white, my teeth clicked against each other, and I couldn't stop them. B-17s were announcing the end of the world.

At 12:50 on February 23rd, 1945, Kitzingen was completely obscured in a cloud of dust that rose several thousand feet into the Franconian sky. The American planes had dropped 2,195 five-hundred-pound bombs and returned to England where they arrived during the afternoon. They hadn't lost a single B-17.

We took the ornaments off the dry Christmas tree. One of the ornaments that had survived was my favorite: a Hexenhaus, the gingerbread house of the witch in Hänsel and Gretel, shimmering with silver and gold, browns and reds. As I wrapped it and put it into its box, it looked vulnerable, out of place. I had doubts there would ever be a Christmas again.

Easter 1945 fell on April 1. The night before it was rumored that Americans were only hours away! Frau Riedel whispered into my mother's ears that we should have some white sheets ready in order to surrender. Gertrude said we would all be shot as traitors; we had secret weapons that would turn the enemy away. But nobody bothered listening to her. My mother took out two clean sheets. Frau Riedel said old bedsheets would do; the Americans wouldn't know the difference. A white sheet was a white sheet!

While they discussed white sheets for surrendering, the German Army moved out, and the Air Force School followed. While the gray army trucks rolled down the Landwehrplatz, American planes roared out of the sky and shot at them. Some of them missed their targets and shot into our bedroom windows; a bullet went through a Bavarian landscape into the wall. Nothing was safe anymore, my mother said. Little boys and old men were being drafted to build barricades to hold off the Americans! My sister Ilse was ordered to sit in foxholes outside the city and watch for enemy paratroopers.

While I sat in the cellar and ate an Easter egg we had colored with onion skin by candlelight, I listened to people talk about Americans who threw hand grenades into cellars where children and women were hiding. The Americans were going to pulverize us! When we woke up on April 2, we were alone in the old gendarmerie; the Ritters, the Kluges and the Riedels had fled to the countryside. The widow and her half-orphans had been abandoned to the Americans who were coming to loot the city.

At one a.m. on April 5, my mother said that we had to act now, our secret weapons weren't going to turn the Americans away anymore.

We marched into our garden; my mother first with a shovel; then Ilse with two big cooking pots, Gertrude carried a box, and I brought up the rear with our pressure cooker. We were going to bury the Third Reich. We dug a hole under the pear tree as the night burned in a slow fire. We wrapped a blanket around the box with our silver. The looting Poles and Russians weren't going to get that. Then we buried two pots so that we would have something to cook in after the looters were gone. Ilse dug a second hole for our pressure cooker. It had been used for steaming potatoes since my parents' marriage. Now it held our insurance paper, savings books, ancestors' chart, and my father's documents. In the center of the cooker lay my mother's jewelry including an eighteenth-century silver cupid holding a garland of flowers on an oval brooch. My father's medals were with the angel.

From the pear tree we went toward the ducks. The ground was slippery and wet because the ducks always splashed water from the pond. We dug another hole, one we wouldn't open up again. The ducks awoke and flapped their wings. My mother threw in her party membership book, then Ilse's, then my father's. Party buttons followed, black swastikas on a brown ground. A large knife with the SS-emblem, all of my father's decorations with swastikas on them, even some of his epaulettes and then a small caliber gun we always kept in my father's desk. Then we covered the Third Reich. We stomped on the ground, while the night sent out fiery signals, thunder and lightning, and the Americans hurled shells whistling through dark spaces over us. Then we ran upstairs and tied a white sheet to the flagpole.

Our capture came fast; one moment we were citizens of Hitler's Reich, and in the next we belonged to a new world. The Americans swept in silently through the garden, surrounding us and pushed us outside. With our hands against Frau Kolb's red walls, the soldiers searched us for weapons. The soldier who had climbed the Beyers' wall frisked me. My heart was beating hard under clothes that exhaled the dank air of the cellar. He didn't notice. He ran his hands up and down my sides and inside my legs with fast expertise and went on to Gertrude. Meanwhile, the Americans stormed the office and smashed the portrait of Hitler over my father's desk which we had forgotten. They broke open the gun cupboard and smashed the guns over the bannisters. The guns broke, but the monks' bannisters held; then the Americans swept through the apartments. We stood still with our hands in the air, like criminals, my mother murmured.

On April 9, 1945, five days after the fall of Kitzingen, the last B-17 rolled off the assembly line in Seattle. A crucial period of my metaphysical education came to an end. My eyes no longer searched the skies for angels in oxygen masks that made my teeth chatter, now I watched the Americans in full daylight stringing out telephone cables along linden square. They spun wire off their large wooden spools with dizzying speed. Out of nothing they created a system of cables, machines, and motors which hummed and emitted lights, and captured voices from the void. The Americans moved with speed, precision, and powerful bodies: I fell in love with them.

While the German Army still fought not far from us, and while German jets appeared in the sky to strafe the Americans, I became a traitor to the Reich: the Third Reich was on the garbage pile in the hall. We dug out Göring and Hitler from the sand and tore them apart. Pieces of their portraits lay on top of the shattered plaster and broken rifles. Someone added the red-inked war chart from the office. The war was over; it was a dusty and unimportant part of the past.

The Americans had power. They had machines that conquered everything; they were green like their uniforms. Their bodies and machines blended into one. And the Americans had food. Their field kitchen was behind our garden wall in the hospital yard. We smelled American food from our garden. Their kitchen warmed up the air

77

and made it fragrant; abundant food being cooked and a soft edge of burning kerosene with which they fired their stoves. Life was on the American side of the high wall; Germans lined up with pots and pans each afternoon to get leftovers from the Americans who poured the food down the drain before their eyes. Frau Beyer begged for coffee grounds and got them. We brewed coffee with them over and over again until only thinly colored water was produced.

My sisters came into the garden wearing bathing suits. They stretched out in the garden chairs under the pear tree to soak up the warm April sun and get rid of their cellar paleness. Anneliese and I climbed down from our tree and visited the ducks, who stabbed their beaks into the water, and nibbled at wilted cabbage leaves. I heard a whistle then another. The whistles had two tones, a higher one and the second one descending a register. An American soldier was sitting on top of the wall waving at my sisters who wouldn't bat an eye. Two other soldiers, drinking out of a green wine bottle, joined him. They hooted and shouted. My sisters remained immobile in their chairs. We looked back and forth between my sisters and the soldiers on the wall, transfixed in our spot between two cabbage patches. Why didn't my sisters answer or respond? I was tempted to do it for them. But the soldiers didn't even look in our direction. My sisters in their polka dotted bathing suits, Ilse's red and white, Gertrude's white and pink, looked like two giant geraniums against the brownish walls of the old monastery.

The wall was filled by soldiers. They stood on the wall or sat astride on it, dangling their legs into our garden. They waved, shouted, whistled, and every time my sisters wiggled a toe the wall of soldiers howled like an undulating olive-green wave. One soldier had even climbed on top of the hospital roof and sat perched on one of the stone balls that ornamented the corners of the roof. The whistles and shouts produced no reaction from my sisters. They started to throw things into our garden. Packs of chewing gum—green, yellow, and white, fell into the dormant flower beds. Dark brown Hershey bars, entire K-rations, cans of peanuts, gull-green cans of peas, beans, peaches, bottles of wine, apple sauce and soups.

Annaliese and I became frantic. We pulled out an old wooden box from underneath the rabbit hutches and flew across the vegetable beds to collect the objects that landed with quiet thuds. A pack of Lucky Strikes sailed across, the biggest prize of all. Red and white. The cellophane felt cool and crisp, and crackled when stroked. My mother, later on, exchanged it for butter on the black market—she always said she could have started an empire with that pack of Lucky Strikes if she had wanted to, but there were already too many crooks around.

Our box was rapidly filling, still my sisters didn't move. We scurried on like excited scavengers. The American heaven had opened. A multitude of American hands kept throwing things in our direction. I knew they weren't thrown for me, but I picked them up. I became my sisters' surrogate, responding because they didn't.

The soldiers on the wall opened bottles of champagne; corks popped in the air. My sisters still didn't move their chairs. One soldier threw an Army boot into the garden. My mother rushed out in her apron, towel in hand, and ordered my sisters inside. We watched her towel dance up and down as she talked to my sisters, pointing at the door. When my sisters finally went inside, the soldiers on the wall let out a howl that made the pear tree shake, then slowly climbed back into their own territory.

I searched every inch of the garden several times following that miraculous morning to make sure I found everything. We had missed chewing gum—Wrigley's and Juicy Fruit in yellow wrappers. When I peeled off the paper and dirt, I found tiny sticky drops on the flat, waferlike gum. Ants had gotten to it. I brushed them off and began to chew. It tasted fresh sweet, and sticky. America smelled like Juicy Fruit gum.

My occupation with the Americans became an obsession. While the German armies still tried to throw back the Allies in the west and north, I surrendered my soul to the conquerors. . . . I embraced their domination with all my heart. I rose for the Americans in the morning and went to bed with them at night. All truth and justice was with them.

When they handed some of us children copies of *Life* magazine with photos of German concentration camps and told us to show them to our parents, I believed them true without the slightest hesitation, although the adults all said it was lies and propaganda. Germans would never do anything like that! I defended the Americans and said they didn't lie! I was the messenger of the Americans and wanted to propagate their truths. When Frau Riedel made fun of me and asked me how I could know the truth, I hurled a single sentence at her! "The Americans said so!"

I lived in a universe of dominating males. There was the cook, a huge soldier who could pick me up with one hand and plunk me into his big pots. There was the "other" whose name I couldn't remember, dark-haired and always drunk in the evenings, he threw bottles against the wall. There was Edward, a mechanic, and Charley who never wore a T-shirt; his name tags rattled wherever he went. Last was Ray, whose name sounded like "*Reh*," deer, in German. In the evening I closed my prayers with "Dear God, protect Father, Mother, Ilse, Gertrude, Edward, the Cook, the Other, Charley, me and Ray!" In this sequence. I had incorporated the Americans fully into my enclosed world, I presented them to God each night, they were my guardian angels when I closed my eyes.

I put Ray last because he was the most important. His name ended my prayer like an exclamation point! I envisioned Ray protecting the rear of those marching in the prayer.

The present and the future belonged entirely to the Americans, to Ray. Sunlight shot through with greens. Ray had chocolate and chewing gum next to the Old Spice on the top shelf of his locker. I was allowed to take what I wanted; Ray took care of me. He had fought the war for me; he battled the Germans for thousands of miles to capture me.

Ray was unpredictable. Some days his generosity and kindness changed into tough meanness; it gave him pleasure to tell me that there was no chocolate, no chewing gum, and I wasn't allowed to check the top shelf from where the smell of aftershave floated down. The top shelf was mine. Ray deliberately and arbitrarily withheld my rights from me. If I tried to force my way to the top shelf, he slapped me on the rear. I didn't question his changeable nature; Ray was the supreme ruler of the universe; he had the right to do what he wanted. His moodiness challenged me to challenge him.

I pulled myself to the top shelf; there was a Hershey bar although Ray had said there wasn't. He had lied; he was lying on his bed, listening to music and reading a Dick Tracy comic book.

When he saw me, Ray pulled me down from the locker and slapped me on the rear. Then he went back to his bed. His punishment was brief and disinterested for the moment. It pushed me to challenge him further. I defied Ray again, he slapped me again.

Ray had a novel way of punishing. He slapped me with the back of his hand rather than with the inside. It reminded me of the way Americans often sat on their chairs in the garden; in reverse; facing the back of the chair.

Outside across the fence Frau Riedel hung up her laundry in our part of the garden; she, a ritual of the known, moved in a dreamlike, padded dimension, cushioned by the ordinary. I moved in a superior space, in the arms of the glittering magnificent constellation of Orion, the hunter. I hurled English words I didn't understand at him, asshole, cocksucker, as soon as Ray let me loose. He ran after me, caught me at the door or in the hallway and carried me back to his room. The corridor was empty, soldiers' voices drifted up from the big hall downstairs. Ray's identification tags jingled. I stared at them in ecstasy. "That's a bad word!" he said, "a bad, bad word. . . . " I supplied Ray with a reason for my own punishment. His hand came down hard on the word "bad."

Ray had stopped laughing. He punished harder after each escape. Ray hit me with his whole hand, on my head, my sides, my chest, my legs, wherever he wished, wherever passion sought its goal.

It was evening when my mother made her discovery. I was getting ready for bed when she screamed, "Jesus Maria!" and pulled off my clothes. While she ran downstairs to get Frau Riedel, I looked at myself in the mirror; dark colors, Ray's colors, ran from my buttocks upwards in all directions over my body. Greens, blues, reds, sunsets, sunrises, whole landscapes with verdant gardens covered my body.

Frau Riedel poked her finger into my buttocks. I could feel her breath on my skin. I didn't say anything. They asked me who had done it, I said it didn't hurt, I didn't know. The two women screamed and slapped their hands together in front of their bosoms; they looked like madonnas beseeching heaven. When I finally told them that Ray had done it, I didn't mean to betray him.

In spite of the curfew, the two women marched me off to the Jewish School that had been occupied by American officers. In front of an officer in light pants and a brown jacket, I had to let my pants down once again. Frau Riedel insisted that such a crime must be punished! I cringed, I couldn't look at the officer. He walked around me and bent down to get a good look. Then he winked at me through his rimless glasses. I said it didn't hurt. I failed to understand the word "crime" used by Frau Riedel. I fell silent and refused to say anything more.

Nothing came of the incident. I was told to stay away from the Americans, but they were an incurable addiction. I went back to Ray.

He gave me a Hershey bar when he was in a good mood, ruffled my hair, and slapped me on the rear when he was in a bad mood. Nothing had changed.

Not long after the fall of the Third Reich, we played in the moat. A girl from Silesia, another from East Prussia, Heinz from the square, Manfred, son of an elderly couple, Georg, a widow's son who lived two blocks away, and I. The girl from Silesia had a white ribbon in her hair. We, the remnants from the destroyed Reich, roamed over the garbage of the Reich.

We pulled objects from the dump and feverishly started to build a tent on top of the grassy hill of the technical emergency service. We felt compelled to build a house, a sort of nest in the middle of the ruins, as if we wanted to triumph over chaos. We spent hours on it, polished it with our imagination into a magnificent structure, and crawled into it. It was hot inside, with earthworms crawling over the rotting, moldy tarpaulin we used as a roof.

It was a warm and blue day. The Americans were across the street from us. Their noises and music floated over us, we felt secure and sheltered in our own creation.

But war wasn't over yet; it was watching us with half-open eyes. Our childish fantasy contained a profound shock; death was coiled in is center like a spring waiting for a trigger. We triggered our own destruction. We had built a home over a discarded grenade, probably of German origin. The explosion was so loud I instantly turned deaf; in the ensuing silent space, the tent was lifted into the air and scattered with lightning speed as if God's mouth had blown on it.

I registered the first sight of color again: it was blood oozing from between the legs of the Silesian girl and staining the light material of her dress. She was lying on her back, moaning with closed eyes; her white ribbon looked like a squashed butterfly in her hair crushed against a rock. The other girl was crumpled against her bleeding friend. I stood up in the subsiding turmoil. I saw the girl's blood as a sign of life. Heinz was lying on his back, his limbs relaxed in curious angles. His face was covered with large fragments of the shell that had gone under his skin. He had one large gash on his left cheek. Manfred was a blackened heap turned into itself. One of his legs was missing; his eyes were wide open as if they were still trying to understand the sudden reversal of fate; they were staring straight into the sun without blinking. Manfred's skull was open, and spongy matter was dripping down his temples. Georg, the widow's son, was sitting on the ground with his head in his hands; he screamed while blood poured down his head. His body looked burned and sooty. I had two selves, one dazed, one sharply conscious. I registered the Americans jumping out of every window of the gendarmerie's ground floor. Jeeps and an ambulance came streaming toward me as I stood rooted to the spot afraid to move as if any movement could destroy my survival. An American soldier reached me and took me up in his arms, but I started to struggle and scream. All I wanted to do was find my mother. I wrestled myself out of his arms and ran home, not conscious of the blood that covered my body. My mother met me at the door, white as a ghost; she stared at me as I told her breathlessly with a mixture of horror and pride, that Heinz and Manfred were dead.

I was euphoric; people looked at me like a hero, I was the only one who walked away from the bomb! People stopped talking on the square when I passed and pointed at me. I allowed myself to be flooded with light; it drowned out Heinz and Manfred who had been consumed by the black ball of fire.

One morning it was all over. On a late summer day in 1945 (the leaves of the Landwehrplatz had already lost their early green), I came downstairs as usual and found the square empty. I had come down for Ray and found a gaping space. The doors and the windows of the Beyers' part of the old monastery stood wide open; the Americans had left. Winds blew chewing gum wrappers along the street.

I stood alone under the old linden trees and watched the last trucks leave. They gunned their motors as they went up the hill to get onto the Federal Highway 8, to disappear forever from my life. Edward, the Cook, the Other, Charley, and Ray left me behind without the slightest warning. They abandoned me, disappeared into the night and fog. The only proof that they ever existed was in my loving memory.

CHAPTER FIVE

# Against Two Enemies

*A Finnish Family's Odyssey*

*Stina Katchadourian* spent the war years between Finland and Sweden. Finland itself was trapped between aggressors, and fought wars against both Stalin's Soviet Union and Hitler's Germany. The first war, known as the Winter War, began with the Soviet attack on Finland in 1939 and lasted only several months. A second war against the Soviet Union, fought by the Finns with the aid of Nazi Germany and known as the Continuation War, lasted from 1941 to 1944. To maintain as much of its independence as possible, Finland was then forced by the Soviets to switch allegiances, and fought a third war in the Arctic against the Germans. Squeezed between Russia and Germany, Finland ultimately came out of the war on the side of the Allies.

Stina's memoir, *The Lapp King's Daughter*, recounts her family's travels to stay ahead of the destruction. While her father, Lale, was commanding troops on the Russian front, Stina's mother, Nunni, managed to move Stina and her sister, Maj, as well as their nanny and housekeeper, Riikka, from Helsinki to the Finnish province of Lapland and then to Sweden. This memoir offers a rare view of Finland's tribulations during World War II. It is also a tribute to the human spirit incarnated in Stina's parents and others who demonstrated courage and decency in the face of countless man-made horrors. In Stina's account, we see a girl scrambling to maintain humor and creativity throughout the ordeal of constant displacement.

AT THE END of my fifth year of life, I knew two things for certain: as long as I could see Nunni at her desk writing a letter, my Papi was alive. He was gone to something called The Front, to scare the Russians away. Nunni wouldn't be writing to him if he had died.

And something else was certain too: tonight the Russian planes would appear, because all day, we had Russian weather. The sun was shining from a clear blue sky this cold winter day in 1942, and that was not a good sign. You could tell the grownups were worried; they kept looking up at the sky, and I was allowed to play in the snow briefly, but only if I wore my white snow cape so the Russians couldn't spot me. As I prepared for bed, I made sure my stuffed dog was securely next to me, so I could take him along if we needed to rush down to the air-raid shelter.

Just after midnight, "Hoarse Freddy," the mushroom-like siren on top of our apartment building, started his warning wail. Nunni hurried to wake me, and on came my itchy long stockings, the padded coat, the felt boots. I knew there were three hundred and twenty steps of spiral staircase down to the communal laundry room in the basement that served as our shelter. The door was creaking as family after family made their way in. The air had a musty, stuffy smell as we navigated our way to the back wall through a forest of wooden pillars placed there to prevent the roof from caving in on us in case of a hit.

From time to time, as someone opened the door, we could hear the droning of the planes and the rat-tat-tat of the air defenses. Search lights swept the black sky. There was an explosion, and then another one, closer. I looked at Nunni: how close was that? She smiled at me, and I knew Molotov and Stalin would not find us here, and Papi was out there somewhere to scare them off.

The winter of 1942 was uncommonly cold. Our apartment was freezing. To make her trips to town on the unheated tram more comfortable, my creative mother exchanged some butter for a black sheepskin that she sewed onto the inside of her thinning winter coat.

Finally, spring came with its milder weather and longer days. When young nettles began to sprout, we picked them by the basketful for "spinach" and soup. We gathered dandelion roots and dried them for substitute coffee. We dried raspberry leaves, flowers from the linden trees, and black currant leaves for "tea." And as spring turned into summer we, along with our neighbors, tended our small garden plots of carrots and potatoes, peas and radishes, beets and beans, utilizing every square inch. There was intense cultivation of vegetables and potatoes going on everywhere: even in the city, some open squares and market places were converted into potato patches.

One day, I found my mother at her desk, looking intently at a small pile of gold jewelry. There was my grandmother's watch that she used to wear around her neck on a gold chain. There was a brooch with gold and pearls, and a hatpin with diamonds. Nunni looked at me as she took her wedding band off her finger. "These are going to the military, so that they can buy more airplanes to defend our country," she said, her voice unsteady. In exchange, she told me, she and all the other women who relinquished their wedding rings would receive plain iron ones from the government. Nunni wore hers, like a badge of honor, all her life.

There was one way our parents could have spared us from the perils of wartime: they could have sent us to Sweden. Had my parents asked me to go, I might well have agreed. Sweden sounded good to me. I had met some Swedes, friends of my parents, and the women smelled of perfume and had fancy clothes, although they spoke a funny, sing-song kind of Swedish. I had seen pictures of the Swedish royal family in magazines. A King, a Queen, Princesses! And I had heard stories: there was no war there. There was peace. You could have as much chocolate as you liked, and oranges. You could buy new shoes by just walking into a store. Two of my cousins had been sent there, and several of my friends.

Some seventy thousand Finnish children, however, in one of the largest child transports in history, did go. It was an exodus on the model of the Kindertransports that sent mostly Jewish children to England, away from the Nazis in Germany, Austria, Poland, and Czechoslovakia in 1938 until the outbreak of the war in 1939. Most of the Finnish children were sent to Sweden, four thousand to Denmark and a hundred to Norway.

We were surviving. Thanks to Nunni's and Lale's efforts, and thanks to Riikka's heroics in the kitchen, we were surviving. We were getting used to the nights in the shelter, to the blacked-out city, to the scarcities, even to the fear. And once in a while, Lale came on leave: those days were feasts.

We had left our home twice during the war years: once at the outbreak of the Winter War, and then once again when the Continuation War broke out. We had gotten used to living in new places and to not knowing when we would return. And then we did come back to Helsinki, and although we were afraid of the bombs, this is where we hoped to stay until the war was over. Little did we know that all this was just the beginning of our wanderings.

On a cold December night, as 1943 turned into 1944, we listened to the President's traditional solemn radio address to the people. The apartment was cold as usual. My mother had lit a fire in the fireplace, and now we took turns putting our New Year's "luck"—a piece of tin— in a ladle and, holding it over the glowing coals, watching as the tin melted into a thick, silvery liquid. Then, a quick flick of the wrist over the waiting bucket of cold water as we shouted our name, and the molten tin would solidify in the water: our "luck" for the coming year.

My mother pretended to read good tidings into the shining tin shapes: here is Papi coming home, here is food coming our way, and look! Here is a fancy dress for Maj! But her mood was somber. More soldiers were dying at the front every day and the food situation was growing even worse. Schools, only intermittently in session, were replaced by an effort at "long-distance learning" via lessons published in newspapers. My sister and her friends had to accept the fact that the government had forbidden dancing. They were working hard to collect points for an "iron spade," a small brooch given for civilian work on the home front: harvesting potatoes, collecting firewood, babysitting, helping the elderly. I gathered pine cones for our fireplace. Riikka, in her kitchen domain, where even my mother wasn't always welcome, did her very best to produce tasty meals with whatever little was available. The daily refrain was: finish everything on your plate!

We could probably have continued on in this manner for a while longer. But then, on February 6, 1944, everything changed. On that night, the Russians carried out the first of three large-scale bomb attacks aimed at terrorizing the civilian population of Helsinki. Helsinki's air defenses, however, were prepared for this blitz. A barrage of modern anti-aircraft guns procured from Germany greeted the attacking planes. Nonetheless, one hundred civilians were killed, and the hospitals filled up with wounded women and children.

My parents immediately realized that living in Helsinki was no longer an option. Schools closed, and everybody prepared for the inevitable second round of bombs. On February 8, the head of Helsinki's air defense urged civilians to leave the city. Once again, we packed our bags. This time we headed for Aunt Biggi's and Uncle Bert's summer place, an hour's bus ride east of the city.

Ten days after our arrival at Aunt Biggi's, another wave of airplanes with even more bombs hit Helsinki. The air defense proved effective: of 3,500 bombs, only 130 hit the city and casualties were light. And then, on February 26, came the final, most devastating attack. For twelve hours, wave after wave of planes hit the city. With its buildings destroyed and hundreds of civilians killed and wounded, Helsinki

Stina Katchadourian and her mother, Runa "Nunni" Lindfors, in Helsinki, 1945.

looked like a doomed city. Out in the country during the bombings, my mother and my aunt were beginning to wonder if we had moved far enough away from Helsinki.

It was shortly after that I overheard my Uncle Bert scolding my cousins in white fury. I had never heard him raise his voice before. But this time, he was screaming at them, and Aunt Biggs was staring down at her knitting looking frightened.

"This is simply the most idiotic thing I have heard of! You go straight back and apologize, do you hear? Apologize, and tell them you'll never do anything like this again. I am ashamed of you!"

What had caused all this fury was that, down the road from us, there lived a family who was Jewish. They were acquainted with Uncle Bert and his family and had a son who was the age of the youngest of my cousins. My cousins and two of their friends decided to play a joke on them. They marched down to the front of their house and started belting out the Horst Wessel song, the official anthem of the Nazi party. Someone inside had peeked through the window, recognized my cousins, and called Uncle Bert.

During the spring of 1944, the Soviets and the Finns made some efforts to end the war. But the Finns would not agree to the Soviet demands of unconditional surrender. Finland had hundreds of thousands of soldiers deep in eastern Karelia and on the Karelian Isthmus, and if needed, the country was still capable of raising more troops. Trying to reach a separate peace with the Soviet Union was fraught with risk: how would the Germans react? Finland needed their weapons and their help, and Germany had several divisions of troops on Finnish soil. In addition, the food situation in the country had grown even more severe, and Finland was relying heavily on provisions imported from Germany.

Three days after the Allied landings in Normandy, on June 9, 1944, the Soviet Army staged a massive attack on the Karelian Isthmus. Approximately 450,000 Soviet troops with 1,000 heavy tanks and 10,000 cannon pressed the desperate Finns back toward the west. A thousand Soviet airplanes blasted Finnish positions. This time of year, there was no darkness to hide in, nor any snow or cold to slow the Soviet advance.

In the face of the near collapse of the Finnish defenses, and with the certainly of a renewed attack, there were two alternatives for Finland: fight on, with dwindling resources, or sue for peace before the country was forced to capitulate. Field Marshal Mannerheim, as well as the government, was now inclined to use the lull in the fighting to send a new peace feeler to Moscow.

But before Finland could enter into negotiations, there had to be an official break with Hitler's Germany. This was a Soviet precondition. And not only that: the Finns were to see to it that the German troops on Finnish soil—the whole Twentieth Mountain Army in northern Finland of more than 200,000 troops—would retreat from the country in a matter of two weeks. The timing was to start from the moment the Finns accepted the peace conditions. If the Germans had not left Finnish soil within that period—which was a logistical impossibility given their numbers—then the Finns were to consider the Germans as prisoners of war and take action to detain them.

It was a tall order, but there was no other way.

Before the cease-fire negotiations had gotten under way, my father decided we needed to leave Aunt Biggi's country place and head north once again. But this time we went even further north than we had before. In mid-June, we ended up on a farmstead near the small town of Ylitornio on the river that separates Finland from Sweden, a few miles from the Arctic Circle. Only much later, reading his letters to my mother did I understand why my father had asked us to find a place to live as close as possible to Sweden. Finland, he reasoned, might not have much time left as a free nation. In case the Soviets occupied the country, we could cross the Tornio River into Sweden and freedom. "Give Maj and Riikka written instructions with Svante's address [Svante was a Swedish colleague of Lale's] and phone number in Sweden, in case they have to cross the border without you," he warned my mother.

Lale was not the only one who worried about an imminent Soviet occupation. But even my cautious father could not have foreseen that he was sending his family straight into a future war zone.

Unbeknownst to my mother, three additional passengers snuck in and joined us on that journey to northern Finland, to the Province of Lapland: a pair of red-headed twins, named Gutter and Better, and their little bouncy friend, Anschovinchen Bonscheli. I had made it perfectly clear to my family that they were frequent visitors to our apartment in Helsinki. At times, there had to be three extra place settings at the dinner table, at other times, they simply phoned and long conversations ensued. Gutter and Better played the piano and Anschovinchen composed. Gutter had a tendency to hiccup, Better picked his nose, and Anschovinchen spoke with food in his mouth. They were a handful, and my loud conversations with them caused my sister, six years older, endless embarrassment in front of her friends.

Why should that be so? I wondered. They took up no room. They ate none of the food that was so hard to come by. And they never objected to being woken up in the middle of the night to go down to the air-raid shelter. My three playmates were entirely imaginary, and they filled the void left after my real playmates had been scattered to the winds.

When we arrived at the Ylitornio train station, we were met by the news that the place we thought we were going to was already full of evacuees from southern Finland. Instead, a shy girl at the station from another farmstead motioned us to come with her. We left all our things at the station and walked with her to the farmstead where she lived, a stone's throw from the river that separates Finland from Sweden. The main building was a low, prosperous-looking house on open land, surrounded by outhouses and barns. I liked the place immediately: there was a dog, a chicken-coop, and I could see three cows and a horse grazing on a field nearby.

I was excited: we were now in Lapland. I knew something about Lapland, since Nunni and Lale had made several trips there to ski cross-country on the treeless, windswept Lapp mountains the Scandinavians call fells. It was not a country, but rather a geographical area made up of the northern parts of Finland, Sweden, Norway and Russia. We were now in the Finnish Province of Lapland, which constituted almost a third of the entire country, stretching north all the way to the Arctic Sea. I also knew that Lapps lived in Lapland, and that they were different from Finns. They were the original inhabitants of Finland, who had gradually been pushed farther and farther north as the Finns moved in. They had their own language and they preferred to call themselves Sami. They were the people of the wide open spaces who kept reindeer, who had colorful costumes, who lived in tepee-like dwellings called kotas, and who—so Nunni told me—knew many of nature's mysterious secrets. I was thrilled to be in Lapland, but I didn't see any Lapps in Ylitornio. The family who took us in were Finns. The real Lapps lived farther north, Nunni said. In summer they were up on the open tundra, on the fells, guarding their reindeer herds.

As soon as we got to the homestead, Gutter, Better, and Anschovinchen Bonscheli vanished into thin air. The Finnish-speaking family who took us in had five flesh-and blood children, and other children lived nearby. The land, bathed in the constant daylight of late June, was wide open with fields of barley and wheat, and the waters of the mighty Tornio River, just a five-minute walk from the farmstead, were full of fish. In the north, on the Finnish side, we could see the majestic silhouette of the Aavasaksa mountain, holy to the Lapps and a popular place to watch the setting midnight sun touch the horizon and then, as if pulled up by a magic string, start to rise again.

My father, who was in Helsinki on leave, wrote to Nunni: "I'm sending you a pair of pants to be patched. Wrapped in these pants there is a small saucepan with two eggs, surrounded by many layers of paper. Write immediately and tell me if they survived the journey. If there is time, I'll also send you another package with two cucumbers, some radishes and rhubarb, and the white enameled milk pail filled with salted Baltic herring."

"It's beautiful here," my mother answered. "The light in the morning, when I'm the only person about, is so luminous that I sometimes stop right in my tracks. The cows recognize me already and come when I call them—they even know their turn to be milked. Afterwards, when I walk home along the footpath with the steaming milk, I feel so at peace with nature, and I love you with all my homesick heart."

The eggs didn't make it, though. When a second package with one dozen eggs arrived with six of them broken, and smelling, my father stopped the egg shipments.

Even a child, however, could not help noticing that something was wrong those last days of June and early July. Each day, trains were arriving from the Karelian front to the small Ylitornio railway station, and coffin after coffin was unloaded onto the platform. It was hot, and if there was a wind from the direction of the station, it carried a stench with it. On those days, my sister used to sit on the stoop and cover her nose with a handkerchief. She had gone to the station on her bike to fetch the mail, and she told me sternly not to go near there.

"You won't like it. There are coffins on the platform, and they stink."

"How do you know Papi won't be in one of those coffins?" I wondered aloud.

"Because he promised us that he would come back home, silly," my sister assured me.

The church bells were ringing day and night, calling people to funerals. The coffins needed to be buried quickly. Some bore the inscription: "Should not be opened." My mother, in her black skirt and white blouse, bicycled from one funeral to another, and made condolence visits to widows, drinking the bitter-tasting coffee substitute with them in grieving silence. "They are amazing, these women," she wrote to Lale, "the way they manage everything on their farms in the absence of their husbands or sons. They talk about the casualties with such quiet dignity. Last Sunday, eight funerals and the church so full that people were left outside."

The local population had greeted the German troops who arrived in Lapland in the fall of 1940 with a certain amount of suspicion. Few foreigners ever ventured into this vast and sparsely populated area. What precisely were these strangers there for? How long were they going to stay? But over time, as the contacts between the German soldiers and the Finns multiplied, the Finns came to feel more at ease. After all, they knew they needed help against the common enemy, the Soviets, whose raids across the border in the northeast had caused thousands of locals to flee their villages in terror. Many of the northern Finns regarded the German soldiers as a reassuring presence. And there was an enormous number of them: by the time the whole Twentieth Mountain Army was in place with its 220,000 men, it had more than doubled the population of Finnish Lapland.

Here in Lapland under the midnight sun, all this translated into an uneasy coexistence, lasting for three years, from which both parties drew some benefits. The Germans had money, with which they bought reindeer meat and other food, firewood, and hay for their horses from the Finns. They hired them, and paid them handsome wages. They rented houses and rooms from them, and leased land to construct barracks. With the Germans came improvements in the local infrastructure of roads and electricity. Buildings were repaired, German vehicles were used to transport firewood. German horses were lent to help with plowing and sowing. German gas helped keep Finnish vehicles on the roads. The Lapp economy, considering this was wartime, was doing well. In contrast to Norway, where the German troops were an occupying force and generally hated by local population, in Finland they were urged to behave as "guests."

But there were frictions as well. Problems arose mainly over women. The Germans and the Finns may have been "a brother people," but in the name of racial purity, the Nazis discouraged German soldiers from entering into intimate relationships with Finnish woman. Still, with their men folk gone to war, and the young Germans far from home and lonely, things were bound to happen. Many Finnish women lost their hearts to German soldiers, who were more than happy to forget the rules. For a young Finnish woman, a job with the German forces was frequently a job in name only: it was a life of parties and alcohol and access to food and clothing and travel with troops, a life far more exciting than her existence in an isolated village in the Lapland wilderness had ever been. There was little point, people felt, in trying to hide this behind some job description: if a local girl was seen socializing with a German soldier, what, besides sex, was going on, since they didn't even share a common language? If she was unmarried, the authorities tended to look the other way. In wartime, what would you expect? They came down harder on married women. A married woman with loose morals in Lapland could affect her husband's fighting spirit at the front, and that was dangerous. "It is regrettable," wrote a Rovaniemi paper, "that the Finnish woman betrays her honor and her country at a time when Finnish men are suffering the hardships and terrors of war at the front."

Few of these relationships ended in marriage. This was partly due to bureaucratic obstacles, and partly to the abrupt end of the whole German presence in Finland. But close to 1,000 children were born to Finnish mothers and German fathers, and stories about these "footprints of the Alpine boots" continued to linger long after their fathers had left the country. Girls named Ilse and Hannelore, boys named Fritz and Ernst were left behind. These Finnish-German children were largely left to grow up in peace, in stark contrast to the 12,000 children fathered by the Germans in Norway whose births the Nazis regarded as a boon for the Master Race—and who were later stigmatized by the Norwegians as symbols of cooperation with the occupiers.

We are on a field raking hay under the scorching August sun. Two German soldiers on leave have joined the farmer and his family to help. I'm taking a break to drink my lingonberry juice in the shade of the haystack and one of them comes to sit next to me. I stiffen and look away; he smiles. He is looking at me, at my long braids. I sneak a sideways look and notice tears in his eyes. He says something I can't understand. He searches his trouser pocket, and shows me a black and white photograph. It is wrinkled and yellowed and the picture of a girl is looking at me: a girl like me, with long braids.

"*Meine Tochter*," says the soldier. "*Verstehst Du? Meine Tochter*," he says and strokes my hair.

I look around. Nobody has noticed. And I decided: this isn't dangerous. But to be on the safe side, I will mention this only to Gutter and Better and maybe to Anschovinchen Bonscheli.

An order to empty Lapland of its entire civilian population of 168,000 people, along with 50,000 cows and other livestock, was issued in early September of 1944. The order originated with Marshal Mannerheim himself. He feared that widespread fighting would break out in Finnish

Lapland between the Finns and the Germans. Before this happened, Lapland's civilians needed to get out of harm's way.

A plan was quickly drawn up for what was to become the largest civilian evacuation ever in Scandinavian history. Part of the population of Finnish Lapland was to move south, into the region of Ostrobothnia. Another part—50,000 civilians—was to cross the border river into northern Sweden. Official permission to receive up to 100,000 Finnish refugees came promptly from the Swedes, a permission all the more remarkable since Sweden already had taken in thousands of Finnish children, wounded Finnish soldiers, refugees from Nazi-occupied Norway and Denmark, Jewish refugees from central Europe, as well as refugees from the Baltic states. No one could tell when, if ever, these new refugees would be able to return.

The evacuation order changed everything. From farmstead to farmstead, from village to village and town to town, officials on foot, on bikes, and in the few available cars fanned out to spread the word: pack your essentials, food for a day or two, and get going. Now people started talking. Even my friends were wondering: how was this possible? Do we really have to leave our homes and our beloved Lapland, maybe forever? Between sips of coffee, the farmers mumbled: Who will take over? The Germans? The Russians? What will happen to us?

At the end of September our farmer and his wife gathered all the furniture in their living room and ferried it halfway across the river to an island, where they hid it in a barn. Refugees continued passing by, and I made it my business to sit by the window and count the skinny cows as they lumbered by on the wet dirt roads, their bones showing under their mud-stained hides. Nunni, Maj, and I gathered in our room and wrote to Papi for his birthday on October 1. I drew a bowlful of blueberries and printed: "Hope you get some of these. Kisses." My sister said, "Papi, dear 46-year-old. It's okay here, but please let me come home 'cause I want to go to school, you don't want an uneducated daughter who doesn't know what 2 + 2 is, do you? I'll even bike home if I have to!"

So far, there had been no hostilities between the Finns and the Germans. In the evenings, as we waited with our suitcases for the order to leave, the adults were cautiously optimistic. Maybe there really would be an orderly German retreat? Maybe there wouldn't be any fighting after all? Maybe the Finns and the Germans would indeed have the "pretend war" that my mother had wished for, and we would be able to return home?

We were packed up and ready to go. Normal life in Lapland had ground to a halt. Schools were closed. Like pawns in a chess game, everyone waited while the Germans and Finns contemplated their next move.

There was to be no "pretend war." Despite top-secret negotiations in Rovaniemi with the Germans about an orderly retreat, the Finnish military command realized that it faced a stark choice: either do what the Russians wanted and fight the Germans, or risk an open, potentially disastrous conflict with the Soviet Union. On September 20, the Soviet leading newspaper *Pravda* published an ominous article with a warning to Finland: "The main question is the immediate fulfillment of the peace conditions the Allies have presented to Finland. A week has already passed since the government of Finland should have started to disarm the Nazi forces in order to deliver them as prisoners of war to the Soviet Union, but up to this point, not a single Nazi soldier in Finland has been disarmed or extradited."

As the September darkness deepened and the roads got muddier and the icy winds whistled day and night, the whole population of Finnish Lapland was on the move along the winding roads: the refugees with their cattle trudging south and west, followed by army units on foot, some of whom would end up walking close to 1,000 miles to the Norwegian border. The Finnish army was following north on their heels—and the Soviets on their side of the border were getting ready to pounce westward for the fight with the Germans over the Petsamo nickel mines.

On September 28, while we were still biding our time on the farm, the first real battle took place between the Germans and the Finns. We didn't even know it was happening. The local radio had stopped, the German radio was unreliable, and we couldn't get Radio Sweden very clearly. And no mail was getting through.

Starting in 1941, the German influx had created a second boom in Rovaniemi. Almost every other person in Rovaniemi was German, and there was a great need for local labor and know-how. Whole barrack towns had to be built to house the German military. They established their own military hospital. There was a German officer's club, a German bakery, a bookshop and a library. They built new roads and improved existing ones. To do all this and much more, they needed local labor, and the Germans paid well—sometimes double the wages compared to the rest of the country. Despite the fact that the German alcohol made Rovaniemi into the crime capital of Finland, the local populace had never had it so good.

And now, it had all come to an end.

At this point, the fate of Lapland's capital hung in the balance. Here was a chance for the Finns to surround the German troops in Rovaniemi and deliver the prisoners of war the Russians so hotly desired. The streams of refugees had moved on. But the Finns did not advance fast enough. By the time they got close, the Germans had begun, with typical thoroughness, to make preparations for blowing up the town.

They started by blowing up their own depots and barracks as early as October 7, and moved on a few days later to systematically burn most of the buildings in the town. From the slopes of the hills surrounding Rovaniemi, Finnish officials watched in horror as explosions and fires reduced the capital of Lapland to ashes. For five days, the arctic night was as light as day. The last building to be set on fire, just before the Germans withdrew, was the local church. By the time the Finnish troops got there, on October 16, 1944, what had been the center of Lapland was a smoldering, heavily mined pile of rubble with only a dozen buildings left standing.

On October 3, there was still no evacuation order for us in Ylitornio, though everybody knew it was imminent. The Germans were rapidly approaching. Nunni decided to take matters into her own hands. "I'm going to take you across the river," Nunni announced to us in a calm voice as she packed the last of our belongings. "We're going to row over to Sweden."

Our farmer had a large wooden rowboat down by the river. We all climbed in and I sat down next to Riikka. The farmer grabbed one pair of oars, my mother another. I was looking back at the farmhouse as it receded during the half-hour it took us to cross with our heavy load. Riikka was crying and it startled me; I had never seen her cry before. My sister and my cousin both looked somber. No one spoke a word. I worried about all the animals we had to leave behind. I trusted Nunni would take us somewhere safe. She always had. But the new foal, the cows, the horse Erkki?

The oarlocks creaked as Nunni and the farmer dipped their oars in unison into the gray water. I turned around and looked ahead. I could make out a barn and a few houses on the Swedish side. So far, no sign of the land of chocolate and oranges, but as the rowboat touched the shore, I saw Nunni and the farmer smile at each other, in relief.

Nunni and the farmer's family were taking a risk. We crossed into Sweden unofficially, without passports or visas—an act that could have gotten us shot on [the German commander] Rendulic's orders. But she was counting on the help of some of Lale's contacts in northern

Sweden, who had written to him offering help. This was not the time to worry about papers.

There was a small village by the name of Alkullen on the other side. It was swarming with refugees like us, all looking for places to spend the night. Nunni was able to rent, from a friendly Swedish couple, a small attic room that we shared with twenty-five strangers, while we stored our boxes and luggage in a barn. Most of us slept on the attic floor.

A small note to my father from Nunni, handwritten in pencil with miniscule letters, gives a hint of what these days must have been like for her. Once on the Swedish side, she came down with a severe tooth-ache. Unable to endure the pain any longer, she left us in the attic room and bicycled to a country dentist in a nearby village. Before she let him examine her, she told him she had only a few Swedish crowns and asked him not to do anything expensive. After a look, the dentist gave her an anesthetic and extracted the tooth. When he told her there would be no charge, she broke into tears.

For two more days after we had crossed to Sweden, while Maj, Riikka, and I waited in the attic room in Alkullen, my mother rowed back and forth across the river to Finland. She couldn't leave the farmstead's cows, she explained; she had to cross the river to milk them until she could arrange for them to be ferried over to the Swedish side. I remember looking at her in the rowboat as the sound of the oars faded.

When the official evacuation order for the population of the Tornio River valley arrived several days later, we were already in safety in Alkullen. But where would we go now?

The gates to the Swedish Paradise finally cracked open when we entered the apartment of my father's Swedish colleague, Uncle Axel Elgstrand, in the northern town of Luleå. Since we had crossed the border on our own, we had avoided the time-consuming chaos of the official crossing stations into Sweden, with their obligatory health inspections and often humiliating delousing saunas and steaming of clothing that thousands of Finnish evacuees entering Sweden had to endure. But it also meant that we, in contrast to them, had no papers. In the eyes of the Swedish authorities, we were stateless persons. Uncle Axel promised to see what he could do to get us visas, or refugee passports. To make this easier, he and my mother set about finding work for her in one of the many Finnish refugee camps in the outskirts of Luleå. My sister volunteered to do her part and write letters for wounded Finnish soldiers who were housed and treated at a nearby school. Uncle Axel was well positioned to help my mother: he had been put in charge of an organization called the Center for Finnish Livestock (Centralen för Finska Kreatur), whose task it was to house and care for the thousands of cows, horses, and other animals that had arrived in Sweden with the refugees from all over Finnish Lapland.

She had found a job as the supervisor of a small refugee camp just outside the town, where her fluency in both Finnish and Swedish were real assets, and where her work on behalf of the refugees would be appreciated by both refugees and Swedish officials alike. So, for the next few months, she lived in a small, sparsely furnished room close to the church housing the refugees. She tried to come and see us whenever she could. Because of the infectious diseases among the refugees, it was not possible for us to visit her.

"Coming to Sweden has been like turning on the lights," Nunni wrote to Lale. "We can finally know what's happening in the world after the black bag of Lapland."

The world was entering the last, cataclysmic phase of World War II, and now we were able to follow events in the newspapers and over the radio. December 1944 and January 1945, we read about the gigantic

Battle of the Bulge in the Ardennes (in Belgium, Luxembourg, and Germany), where American and British forces engaged the Nazi army in one of the bloodiest battles in the whole war.

My drawing sessions at the Elgstrands' kitchen table turned to the production of a four-page occasional newspaper called *Stina's World News*. It had five subscribers (my own family members and the Elgstrands) and it focused on international stories. Since I was spending much time by myself, my imaginary playmates returned. Most articles in the *World News* were signed either by Gutter, Better, or Anschovinchen Bonscheli.

We were enjoying the plentiful food, the warm water, and the heated apartment in Luleå. Riikka and I slept with the downstairs family, and Maj made her bed at night in the Elgstrands' living room. But the warm glow of our first welcome was already beginning to fade. Much as we tried to be polite and inconspicuous, Uncle Axel's sister-in-law, Helga, who ran the household since Mrs. Elgstrand worked in another town, gave us the distinct feeling that we were in the way. "Sweden will soon turn into a poorhouse with all these refugees," she would mutter. As she presided over the dinner table, we noticed she was checking the amount of food we put on our plates. Uncle Axel himself was always warm and friendly but absorbed with the enormous task of organizing the care of the Finnish cows and horses. Maj spent her time babysitting children and assisting hospitalized soldiers with their letters. I was left to my own resources since Riikka had taken a job with another family. Most days, I spent my time drawing and writing at the kitchen table. Going outside was not an option, since my only pair of shoes had worn out.

But one day, Uncle Axel asked my sister for help. The Swedish Crown Prince Gustav Adolf—the future King Gustav VI Adolf of Sweden—and Crown Princess Louise were coming to northern Sweden to tour the Finnish refugee camps. They had also expressed an interest in seeing some of the barracks where the refugees' cattle were kept. That was Uncle Axel's domain, and now he needed an interpreter. My sister was the perfect person: bilingual and presentable. Needless to say, she readily consented and a few days later, after many sessions of practicing curtsies—was this too low, not low enough?—Uncle Axel and Maj were off to meet the Royals.

"Oh my God," was all she could say after she returned. "Oh my God." It turned out that just as the Crown Princess was asking her a question in one of the narrow temporary cowsheds, a cow had lifted its tail and sprayed the unsuspecting Crown Princess's fur coat with a shower of dung.

"Luckily," my sister said, "the fur was the same color as the cow shit. But I almost died. You should have seen the attendants trying to wipe it all up with their white handkerchiefs."

I spent much of the next day trying to draw a picture of the cow spraying the Crown Princess. At one point, Aunt Helga passed by and asked what I was drawing.

"A cow shitting on a Princess."

Aunt Helga, who was a staunch royalist, was not amused.

In early November, our living situation with the Elgstrands became critical. "The more I get to know Helga, the less I like her," my mother confessed to Lale. "She is so cold and 'correct'—and her polish is skin deep. My soul shivers in her presence." One day, Helga forbade me to draw at the kitchen table, and the final straw for my mother was when Riikka confessed to her that Maj and I were sometimes going hungry during the day. Nunni arranged for Maj to move in with another family who had a daughter her age, for the ostensible reason that she needed company, and she was also allowed to attend the daughter's school. Riikka's job with the Swedish family came to an end, too. Nunni realized that the family she worked for was taking advantage of her with their endless parties and dinner dishes, and paying her very little. She found a new family for the two of us, the Bergströms, who treated us very well.

One morning in November, Riikka left me by the gate of the Luleå Elementary School. "Remember, it's second grade, and be sure to curtsy when you shake hands with the teacher and tell her your name." Bewildered and shy, I found my way into the four-story red brick building. What a difference from the one-room schoolhouse in Ylitornio! I had never seen so many children in one place.

My tenure in second grade was short. The teacher decided to test my reading skills, and asked me to step up in front of the class. Then she gave me a book, opened it to a particular page, and said, "Read."

The letters danced around on the page. I saw Joseph, and Mary, but they refused to sit still in a sentence. There was a deep silence in the class, and some giggles, and then the teacher asked me to sit down. After class, she called me and said: "I think it would be best if you started in first grade."

We were going to spend Christmas with the Elgstrands, and they tried their best to help us have a real holiday away from home. We decorated our tree with candles and sparklers. Food was plentiful: a big baked ham, pickled herrings, beet salad. The house smell of mulled wine and gingerbread. But I missed Lale. For Nunni, his absence and her deep worry about Finland were almost too much to bear, but she never let us know how she felt.

When I returned to school after Christmas break, three classmates met me in the corridor.

"What did you get for Christmas?" they asked.

"A flannel nightgown," I said proudly. Strictly speaking, it was true, but to my great sorrow the nightgown had gotten lost and probably thrown away with the wrapping papers. "And crayons and paper."

My classmates were not impressed. "I got a bicycle," said one of them. "Red. My dad gave it to me. Where is your dad?"

I was starting to dislike the drift of our conversation. I decided to make a pre-emptive move.

"I don't need a bicycle. My dad is the King of the Lapps and where we live we have a thousand reindeer and always get pulled everywhere in sleds."

"You're the Lapp King's daughter?" they asked, slowly.

"Yes, and my Dad's been very busy with Christmas and all. He loans some of our reindeer to Santa Claus and his elves."

"I don't believe you. It's a sin to lie."

"I'm not lying. I'll show you a picture tomorrow."

The next day, I brought a picture of me in a Lapp costume that Nunni had taken in Ylitornio.

"Here," I said. "We don't wear crowns in Lapland, like your king. Just hats like these. Except for royal occasions, when we wear black berets."

"Royal occasions?"

I pulled out a newspaper clipping. In it, my sister is standing next to the Crown Prince and Crown Princess of Sweden who are visiting a Finnish refugee camp. She is wearing a black beret.

"This is my sister. She is the Lapp King's other daughter."

There was a long silence.

"Would you like a chocolate?" one of the girls asked.

Things at school got much better after that.


On April 12, 1945, the radio reported that President Franklin D. Roosevelt had died, and *Stina's World News* hurried out an extra edition with the additional news that Roosevelt had been succeeded by Harry S. Truman. On April 25, the last German troops left Finnish territory.

Nunni now started packing everything Lale had sent us: our skates, our skis and poles, our bike. Into wooden crates it all went:

our clothes, our books and journals, our pots and pans, my doll and stuffed dog. We had good reason to rush: since the bridges to Finland had been destroyed, we needed to leave while the ice covering the border river was strong enough to carry us in a car across to the Finnish side.

After class, I told my teacher, a very kind lady. She seemed genuinely sorry I was leaving, and said the whole class would come to see me off at the railroad station.

"But we are leaving very early," I said, overwhelmed at the thought. "So that we can get over to the Finnish side before it gets dark." Nunni had explained the whole thing and it sounded very easy to me.

"We'll be there anyway," my teacher said.

And on that morning, there they were, my whole class, gathered on the platform in the morning darkness as we arrived with all our things. The teacher asked for a moment of silence and said:

"We wanted to come and wish you and your family all the best for your journey back home. We wish to sing a song for you, but first we want to give you this as a remembrance of your time here in Sweden."

She handed me a small velvet box. Inside was a delicate silver heart on a thin chain, with an inscription: "Stina, Luleå, April 21, 1945."

It was the first piece of jewelry I had ever owned.

"Now children," my teacher said and raised her arms. "Let's sing for Stina and her family." As the locomotive was puffing warm-up clouds of white steam into the chilly morning air, the little cluster of class-mates turned their faces toward me and sang my favorite hymn. . . .

As my classmates were singing the last stanza and I was contem-plating what depth of curtsy would be appropriate for the Lapp King's daughter, I noticed another girl on the platform, right next to my mother.

"This is Ulla Emaus," my mother told me after we had said goodbye to the teacher, the class, and Uncle Axel. "She is coming with us back

Seven-year-old Stina Katchadourian, dressed in
traditional Lapp garb, 1944.

to Helsinki." Then the train whistled and we clambered aboard and my classmates on the platform in their bulky winter coats got smaller and smaller.

I had not met Ulla before, but she was my age and during that long trip down the length of Finland back to Helsinki we sat together, sensing a bond that we could not put into words.

On the platform, beaming at us in the throngs of people milling around the half-ruined railroad station, stood the Lapp King himself. He had kept his promise. He had not come home from the war in a wooden coffin. He had kept our apartment safe. He had steered the Russians away from us, and now he would keep them from invading our country. He had spared us from all evil things. So why then, I wondered after he had given me and my sister a strong hug, why then was my mother crying as he took her in his arms?

# CHAPTER SIX

# Into Exile

*Fleeing Czechoslovakia for England*

Up to the age of twelve, **Susan Groag Bell** lived in Troppau, a provincial town on the northern border of Czechoslovakia. Like the majority of the town's inhabitants, her family spoke German, while many other town folk and the peasants living in the surrounding countryside spoke Czech. As the only child of affluent parents, she lived a very privileged life.

Though her maternal and paternal families were Jewish, Susan's parents had converted to Christianity and Susan was baptized in the Lutheran church. But when Hitler's troops moved into Czechoslovakia in 1938, their Jewish heritage made them prey to destruction. Susan and her mother fled to England, leaving their lawyer father behind with the hope of joining them later. Instead, he was to die in a concentration camp.

In England, Susan's mother worked as a domestic servant—the only employment legally allowed to refugees. Susan had the good fortune of being taken into a girls' boarding school as a non-paying student. She would never forget the kindness of her English benefactors, and repaid them by adopting the best of British virtues: honesty, decency, understatement, and loyalty—all characteristics that come through in her autobiography, *Between Worlds*, from which I have extracted the following pages.

I HAVE PONDERED the reasons for my difficulties in remembering my early life very precisely, even to my inability to impose a chronological order on the years before my eleventh or twelfth. The reason that seems to make the most sense is that the unresolved shock of having so suddenly and drastically lost my stable home and many of the people who created it, on the eve of adolescence, has pushed these events into an unrecoverable haze of nostalgia.

While my father and I used to sit at the small table in the bay in front of the drawing room balcony, he drinking his breakfast coffee and I my chocolate, my mother breakfasted in bed. Afterwards, when he had left for his law office in the Wagnergasse, my mother consulted the cook about the meals for the next two days.

The house in which we now lived belonged to the Baron Sobeck-Skal, who was a member of one of innumerable impoverished minor aristocratic families that abounded in the greater Austro-Hungarian Empire. The baron owed my attorney father a great deal of money for legal services. In a sort of barter system, we therefore lived rent-free in a splendid apartment that occupied most of two floors of the Sobeck-Skals' baroque town house.

One morning in October 1938, as I arrived rather breathlessly in my classroom, I was told to present myself in the principal's office immediately. I could not imagine what scrape I had gotten myself into, but ran up the wide staircase and found two older students, also waiting nervously in front of the headmaster's door. We were ushered in and invited to sit down in front of his imposing desk. To my utter bewilderment, this large red-faced man, unable to meet our eyes, told us between many lengthy pauses and clearings of the throat that it would be advisable for the three of us not to come back to school until further notice. The other two seemed to understand what this was all about. I was completely baffled, but far too intimidated to ask any questions of the headmaster or my fellow pupils.

I went back to my classroom, collected my satchel and books, and started down the steps at the front of the building. The school was parading in the usual circle around the pavement, and as I and the two others who had been in the headmaster's study crossed the circle, a menacing grumbling suddenly erupted into a long drawn-out howl. I became frightened and, starting to run, soon found myself pursued by some of the larger boys from the senior class. They shouted something that I didn't understand and then seemed to lose interest and returned to the parade. The teacher-warders, clustered in the center of the circle, had not moved.

When I returned home in tears, my parent were finally forced to explain what was happening. The Nazis had taken over the Sudetenland. Jews were undesirable in this new state. Although we were not religiously affiliated Jews, all four of my grandparents had been Jewish, and by Hitler's laws we were therefore part of this group. We would have to find a way of leaving the country, probably move to America or Great Britain, and to this end I should soon be learning to speak English. I puzzled about the word undesirable. What did it really mean? And who exactly thought me undesirable? If my school friends thought me undesirable, why had they always been happy to be with me? It didn't make sense.

While this was surely the most disturbing crisis of my young life, my parents' calm explanation soothed the pain and prevented me from panicking about the future. Even more important, they knew how much I enjoyed school and quickly organized another absorbing occupation for me.

The next day I began my English lessons. This meant going to the house of my English-speaking "Aunt" Elsa, who lived at the other end of town, about three times farther away from our home than my school. I had to walk through the town park in the opposite direction from the Gymnasium. On the first day, Martha, our maid, accompanied me to Aunt Elsa's, but I returned alone after the lesson. I had not told my parents about the unpleasant behavior of the older boys at school, and as they seemed to think it safe for me to walk through the park to Aunt Elsa's for the next three months, I saw no reason to burden them with any misgivings.

For the whole of these three months, until my mother and I left for England, we were fed by the owners of several restaurants who were in debt to my father for his legal services. Inns and restaurants were an intrinsic part of my father's life. He had particular corner tables always on reserve at some of them, and specific meals of the week were regularly eaten at these tables. It was one of the great treats of my childhood to accompany my parents, and even more exciting to accompany my father alone, on these occasions. Now, every day, Martha would go to one or the other of these restaurants and return with ready-cooked meals in oven-proof metal containers that sat slotted on top of each other forming a kind of round tower.

Martha was the shield between us and the outside world. She not only helped with the usual household tasks. She went on errands to "the authorities," fetched our food, did the shopping, and negotiated unwelcome visitors who came to the door. She did all this with kindness and an unconscious grace, always remembering to take my little dog, Struppel, with her so that he might have an outing. But her most heroic act, performed "as her Christian duty" regularly every morning for many months, was to go downstairs with a bucket and scrubbing brush at the crack of dawn. Then, in full sight of any passersby, and risking her own personal safety, she scrubbed graffiti like "Jewish swine" from the magnificent front door behind which we were more or less imprisoned.

It was Martha who, one night in December, opened the door at 3:00 a.m. to the group of six SS men who came to search our home. My parents and I were summoned and stood watching, in our dressing gowns, while the men tramped about the place opening cupboards and drawers. On finding my grandfather's Hebrew prayer books, Sabbath candlesticks and menorah in the antique cupboard in our hall, they bundled them up to take them away and announced that we would have to come with them immediately. Then, while we stood there, quite stunned, they went into a huddle in the corner. One of the SS men was the son of Paula Heintz, a close friend of my parents. He had known our family well since he was a little boy. After conferring in their corner, the senior spokesman announced that they had changed their minds, and we could remain at home, but must leave the country by the first of March. Like all other refugees, we would be allowed to take a few personal belongings and the equivalent of one dollar, in cash, out of the country. I have no memory of how, or whether, we returned to bed that night.

Preparations for our stay in England now went ahead at full speed. Friends in Vienna arranged that my mother and I would be ushered into England as guests of an English couple, the McCleans, who were even then wintering at an Austrian spa. This made it possible for us to enter Great Britain on a visitor's visa, the only type of visa still available at this time.

Our old seamstress, Fräulein Schmidt, spent a few days with us making several dresses—far too large—for me "to grow into." I am wearing one of these, a small white and navy check pattern with a white collar, in a photograph taken at my English school about two years later. It is obviously already too small and stretched to the limit across my breasts. My mother packed carefully chosen items into a huge brown trunk, while I insisted on filling a large part of it with my favorite children's books.

Martha offered to look after my father when we had left. She also promised to take care of my dog, Struppel, and my canary, Pipsi, when my father left the country to join us.

The date of our departure was set for the end of January. We were to take the midnight express to Vienna and there to meet our English hosts and procure our visa from the British consulate. My father and

Struppel accompanied my mother and me through the snowy streets to the railway station. I was nervous but buoyed up by the adventure before me. My parents were silent. The train glided in at ten minutes to midnight. We settled in the compartment with our hand luggage, my mother's jewelry hidden among our underclothes. I waved excitedly to my father, as he stood on the platform holding Struppel on a short lead. I never saw him again.

Our situation during the week in Vienna was precarious. We had left my father behind in our hometown, hoping that he would be able to follow us at a later date. Meanwhile, my mother and I were supposedly being escorted to England as the guests of the British McCleans, who had been taking a cure in the mountains near Vienna. We spent many hours waiting in the anterooms at the British consulate. When we were finally ushered into the presence of His Majesty's Consul, we faced a tall, unsmiling man who grudgingly agreed to sign the necessary papers.

Those days in Baroness Ina's Vienna apartment (which Baroness Sobeck-Skal had arranged) have left me with confused and unrealistic memories. We slept in the midst of romantic, almost religious signs of worship of the charismatic empress who in 1896 had been stabbed to death by a fanatic anarchist. Outside, we saw Nazi guards forcing well-dressed Jewish women to sweep the snow from the streets. Wedged between these scenes is the tight-lipped impenetrable face of the British consul who held our lives in the balance.

Two weeks after we arrived in England, my mother, now thirty-eight years old, began her job as a maid to the family of the Reverend Daunton-Fear in Lindfield. This picturesque Sussex village consists of a long curved street leading from a duck pond slightly uphill to the high steepled church.

My mother and I were given a servant's bedroom, which was heated by a gas fire that popped and hissed alarmingly. While it was easier to light than the majestic tiled stoves that had graced our rooms at home, it gave us neither their comfortable warmth nor their aesthetic security. My mother said that since she was now the maid, she was pleased not to have to clean out its grate, nor to carry the coals, but I was appalled because unless one cowered within two or three feet of this gas contraption with its bluish-pink flames, one hardly felt its warmth. Through these cold dark February mornings, we dressed close by the gas fire, warming our garments before to escape their clamminess.

The Reverend Daunton-Fear was a tall, cheerful man with a booming voice and a hearty manner. His family consisted of his elegant, small blond wife, who must have washed her hands constantly as she always smelled of Pears soap, and their two-year-old daughter, whose nurse, Cheggy, soon became a good friend and support to my mother. Mrs. Daunton-Fear had a little sitting room furnished with the first fitted carpet I had ever seen. Both the carpet and the upholstered furniture were a delicate Wedgwood green. It was in this room that all important decisions were made and announced. It was here that I was told that I would be going to St. Clair, a school in nearby Haywards Heath, first as a day girl, and later possibly as a boarder.

The first Saturday morning after we arrived in Lindfield, the vicar drove my mother and me to Haywards Heath to talk to Miss Stevens, the headmistress of St. Clair School for Girls. Miss Stevens talked mostly to me, asking many questions about my life at home and the sorts of things I had done in school before. In fact I was being examined, but in such a subtle manner that I did not understand that I was passing or perhaps failing an examination. I did not then realize that my education at this school would have to be Miss Stevens's gift to me, as St. Clair was her private business and, in order to attend, all other pupils paid fees.

"When would you like to start?" Miss Stevens asked.

As headmistress, Miss Stevens was by no means a nominal head of her school. She was the central and dominant figure. She directed the whole establishment. She chose both the teaching and domestic staff. She interviewed parents and pupils, and she looked after the domestic arrangements and the meals and oversaw the grounds and gardeners. She taught many classes to senior girls. She kissed the boarders good-night and was concerned about their emotional as well as their physical well-being.

After the end of my first term at St. Clair, Miss Stevens decided it would be better if I became a boarder while my mother continued her domestic service in various English households.

One of the first things that happened when I became a pupil at St. Clair was that a uniform was found for me. We wore navy blue wrap-around serge skirts, which gave us more freedom while running, and tomato red jerseys with small collars closed by two white pearl buttons at the neck. Miss Stevens found several mothers of girls who had outgrown their skirts and jerseys and who were willing to pass them on to me. I was told that a uniform had been found for me and was very proud to wear it. As I had never worn a uniform before, this was something rather exciting. I did not realize for a long time that other children had to buy their own. As time went on, the uniform also became extremely useful as it hid the fact that my own clothes were quickly becoming far too small and shabby and we had no money to replace them.

Sometimes I was invited to tea or supper at the home of one of the day girls. On one occasion when I was happily ensconced having tea with my friend Joyce at the other end of town, the house shook and we heard a heavy dull thud. Almost immediately afterwards the phone rang and Joyce's mother said that Miss Stevens was asking for me to come home. I was taken back to school rather abruptly. I found Miss Stevens waiting for me at the gate with her dog Robin in her arms and a bandage on her

Susan Bell (second from right), with her teacher Miss Wiltshire
and fellow students, 1941.

head. Very alarmed I ran to her and she led me wordlessly into the study/
dining room where she had been having her tea with Robin asleep in his
basket. The window was shattered, and broken glass lay everywhere, both
in the room and outside in the garden. A German bomber hit by ack-ack
guns had gone to the ground and exploded with his unused bombs in
the Sussex countryside. Miss Stevens and I survived this incident without too much trauma. But poor little Robin was extremely shaken and
frightened of loud noises for the rest of his life.

Strange as this may seem, this particular bomb incident was the closest I ever came personally to an air raid throughout the entire war. By some mixture of luck and protective foresight on the part of my mother and her friends, I moved about England and Wales several times, always escaping the worst of the bombings in other parts of the British Isles.

The children accepted me in their midst with the least possible fuss and a certain amount of pleased curiosity. Very quickly, I felt at home. I was somewhere in the middle of the school; the little ones, if they thought about me at all, were in awe of a stranger in their midst; the older ones treated me like a little pet; and my own age group soon dealt with me as an equal. At least that's how it felt. I don't know what went on behind the scenes. Perhaps they were all given a lecture on how to behave with a refugee. If so, I was never aware of it. Occasionally, someone asked me why I was a refugee. When I tried to explain about Hitler and the four Jewish grandparents, they would say, "But you aren't a bit Jewish," and while I didn't know what they meant by that statement, it didn't disturb me, particularly because I didn't see how one can wear one's religion on one's sleeve. Much, much later it dawned on me that what these children had meant by Jewish was their image of poor East End Jewish Londoners or a sort of Shylock.

It soon became evident that, except for English language and literature, I was somewhat in advance of the girls of my age, which made up for the liberties I took with their language. At the same time, my mispronunciations and poor prose style and my more than quaint spelling detracted from any cleverness I might have exhibited. One-upmanship was not the order of the day.

In the summer of 1942, Sheila, a fellow student, and I had come as far as St. Clair could take us academically. We both sat for the Oxford school certificate, with Miss Stevens hovering nervously and worrying about our inadequacies. She thought that I would have difficulty in passing the examinations, particularly in history and English. In fact, we both did rather well. Sheila claimed I must be "a positive genius," because I had managed to surpass Miss Stevens's expectations. She herself went on to study mathematics, and I, who wanted to work in the humanities, left for the Croydon High School, where I would be able to prepare for a university in the sixth form.

The year 1942 was a watershed. Three momentous things happened: I passed the school certificate examination, which meant that I had to leave St Clair and Miss Stevens, where I had felt so wonderfully at home; the British government lifted the restriction that forced aliens like my mother to work as domestics; and, unbeknownst to us in England, as we had no means of communicating, the Nazis in Prague sent all Jews to concentration camps. My father was among them. But all that I knew was that the concerned letters he had written to me since we had been in England and that I carried about with me had ceased to arrive.

At the same time that I was planning to move from Haywards Heath to the Croydon High School, my mother was allowed to look for employment that was not domestic. As millions of British office workers had volunteered or been drafted into the military services, the lack of civilian personnel now forced the government to permit "friendly" aliens to work in their place. On leaving school, as a young woman, my mother had worked as a law clerk for her father, and she now considered doing something similar. Her Haywards Heath employer, Mrs. Gold, invited her relatives Leslie and Mary Gunn to take refuge in her home. Uncle Leslie, as I soon began to call Mrs. Gold's cousin, was a large and comfortable solicitor in London. Uncle Leslie was helpful and, through his legal connections, found my mother an eminent firm in Bishopsgate in the City that offered her a position.

Soon afterwards I also went to Croydon to be interviewed by Miss Adams, headmistress of the Croydon High School. The school consisted of a dauntingly large and somber collection of nineteenth-century redbrick buildings. Miss Adams was a small, round woman, briskly efficient and far more formidable than Miss Stevens, whom I considered a member of my family. However, she was kind and seemed to understand the strangeness I felt in these new surroundings. She was also concerned about my living arrangements. The Gunns had offered my mother a room in their house while she got settled in her new job, but they did not have space for me or the complications a teen-aged girl would bring into the household. Miss Adams told me that for several years a Croydon family whose mother and three daughters were all "old girls" had harbored Nazi refugee pupils of the school. The family was eager to take another and would like to meet me.

So began my long-lasting relationship with a fascinating family, the Crags, whose charitable impulses and quirky dry sense of humor were a constant source of surprise and inspiration. The parents, Chris and Iris, owned a large three-story detached house, called Waxham, not far from where my mother now resided with the Gunns in South Croydon. Here they lived with their two youngest adopted children and a motley group of boarders. Their four natural children were fully grown and busy in the working world. But four children had not been enough for Chris and Iris, and they soon adopted others or, as in my case, took them in as foster children. I knew immediately I set foot in Chris and Iris's house that I would enjoy being with them.

One of the greatest problems during the war years, particularly in large, draughty houses like Waxham, was to keep warm. The corridors, bedrooms, and bathroom of Chris and Iris's house were uncomfortably cold, even when we had enough coal or coke to keep the living room fire alight. Chris hated the icy blasts of the unheated corridors and lavatories as much as the rest of us. And sometimes we children were

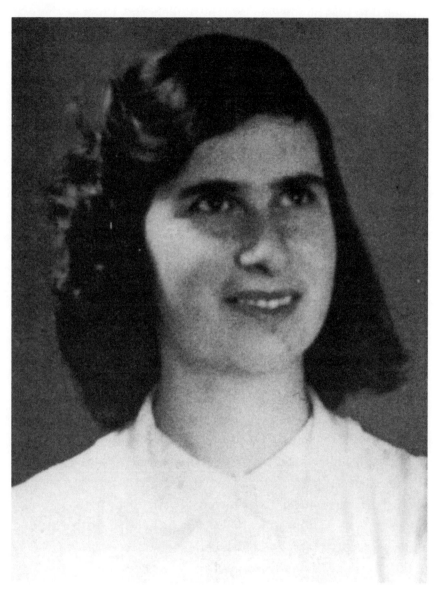

Sixteen-year-old Susan Groag Bell, in England, 1942.

intrigued to find him peeing into the scullery sink when he thought nobody was around. We girls giggled over this feat, and although we adored him, we were quite annoyed with him, both as an adult and as a man, for being able to resort to such an unfair advantage.

In the summer of 1943, the letter I received from the education division of the exiled Czech government in London urged, as on several previous occasions, that I should attend their free, government-sponsored boarding school, which was preparing young Czech refugees like myself to return to their homeland after the war. There we would be urgently needed to help rebuild our country that had for years been under Nazi domination with little or no secondary education. Suddenly this avenue seemed the only sensible course for my immediate future. I felt that I had reached an age when the Czech school sounded not only like an exciting venue, but it also offered an idealistic involvement in creating a better future for our world after the war was won. Further, I would need to know more about Czechoslovakia, where I assumed my future lay, than I could learn in my English schools.

Although I loved living in Chris and Iris's household, I was not enjoying the Croydon High School. While I had performed well in the intimate milieu of St. Clair, I felt out of my depth at the school in Croydon. The latter was very large and the number of pupils in my class seemed overwhelming. I hated the sports, particularly the compulsory games of hockey, from which I always returned home with bruised and massacred ankles. I did not even like the dances to which some of the girls in my form invited me.

So I went to see my mother to discuss the possibility of my accepting the Czech government's proposition. She was dubious on several counts. She was not at all sure that I would feel comfortable surrounded by refugee children, since I had never been involved with refugees as long as I had been in England. Moreover, she herself was about to move in with Chris and Iris as one of their boarders and had looked forward to living under one roof with me for the first time since our leaving Czechoslovakia. However, the more I thought about this new idea, the more it appealed to me, and eventually I persuaded myself and my mother that I should complete my school years at the Czech school rather than in Croydon.

And so at the beginning of the next term, I found myself with about a hundred Czech refugees at Euston Station. The train taking our school from London to Llanwrtyd Wells in Wales was crowded with children and young people, most of whom had known each other for many years. They had all been at the Czech school in Shropshire before it expanded. Now, for the remainder of the war, the Czech government in London had rented the luxurious Abernant Lake Hotel on the Breconshire moors, where it installed its "Gymnasium." Everything was financed by the government—the teachers' salaries and living expenses, as well as the students' tuition and their room and board. This school, which I was about to join, and where I remained for two years from the age of seventeen, was different from anything I had experienced before. First of all, it had a political mission that permeated all our activities; second, it was a coeducational boarding school; and third, it was situated in a luxury hotel in a beautiful scenic resort.

I found that I was to be called Groagovà, short and simple, by the teachers in class and by the other pupils, except by my closest friends. I was shy and somewhat uncomfortable with all these boys and girls who not only knew each other well, but seemed to lapse easily from English into Czech as though both languages were the same. Any Czech I had learned in my early childhood had long since evaporated, and I was forced to begin all over again. Czech, moreover, was the official language of the school. In this language all lessons, homework, games, and most extracurricular activities were conducted. It was clear that we all needed both to speak and to feel Czech, as the aim of the school was to prepare us to rebuild the republic devastated by the Nazis.

Many of the pupils, particularly the older boys, were intensely interested in the military and political progress of the war. As we waited for the teachers to come to the first class every morning, a tense group stood around the fireplace, reading the newspapers, while they debated the latest news. They talked about Churchill, Roosevelt, Stalin, and (Czech President) Beneš, not to mention various generals, admirals, and military commanders, as though they were personal acquaintances. They argued passionately about how these men were handling specific military and diplomatic events.

Although we had found a hospitable haven in England, it was hard to forget Chamberlain's sellout of Czechoslovakia at Munich. There was a strong pull towards both Stalin and Roosevelt among the pupils at the school. While many of them had been forced to leave Czechoslovakia because of Nazi antisemitism, many others, both Czechs and Sudeten Germans, had left their homes because of their parents' socialist beliefs, which naturally produced Soviet sympathies.

Major celebrations commemorated every significant date in the formation and development of the Czechoslovak state. Important members of the exiled government were invited, presented formal speeches, and talked with us and the teachers. On such occasions, the great hotel ballroom was transformed into a political auditorium festooned with flags of the major allies. On the anniversary of the founding of the republic in 1918, the twenty-eighth of October, 1944, for example, the centerpiece on the wall behind the stage was an enormous map of Czechoslovakia with its coat of arms trailing its motto PRAVDA VITEZI (Truth Prevails) above. On the day after Germany's unconditional surrender, on May 8, 1945, the stage was simply dressed with the Czech, British, American, and Russian flags in the shape of a magnificent V for victory.

Immediately, we were told that the Czech government in London was making arrangements for those of us who wanted to return to Czechoslovakia to do so. The government would continue to support us while we were students: the famous Charles University in Prague, soon to be reopened, beckoned intriguingly. So, in late August of 1945, together with most of my intrepid friends, I boarded the American liberator bomber that safely carried me to Prague and the shock of disillusionment.

Before I left England for Prague, my mother had gently and carefully prepared me for the possibility that my father would not have survived. When she told me this, as we were lying in bed in her room one morning, I was unwilling to accept such a reality. Now, in Prague, where all my returning companions were dealing with similar trauma, I too went to the Red Cross offices where information about missing persons would be obtained. As I try to remember this occasion, I find that my mind is a complete blank. I remember many important, and far less important, moments of my life with crystal clarity, but the circumstance of this brutal revelation is as though it had never taken place. It is rather as if some skillful physician (possibly nature herself) had injected me with a strong anesthetic so that I awoke from the operation to a dull ache that remained with me for the time I stayed in Prague, and indeed, for the rest of my life.

I learned some of the circumstances of my father's last years from my childhood friend Hanni, with whom I had spent much of my first twelve years in Troppau. She, and her whole family, had recently also returned to Prague from the concentration camp Theresienstadt, where they had seen something of my father. Theresienstadt (or Teresin) was not an extermination camp, and it housed mostly Czech citizens. The camp had a hospital where Hanni's mother, Tante Boeszi, had a menial job of some kind. She told me that my father had died of pneumonia in the hospital soon after he arrived there. I feared that perhaps she was telling me a comforting white lie, but was too cowardly to delve deeper.

My family—aunts, uncles and cousins—appeared to have been completely wiped out. But also, the Czechoslovakia to which I had returned was a strange and unsympathetic place, and not only because the absence of my family had robbed the country of an atmosphere recognizable as "home." It took a while for me to understand why it was so uncongenial to me.

It gradually became clear to me that as a German-speaking Czechoslovakian citizen, who had been born in the Sudetenland, I was persona non grata. I supposed I should have realized this sooner, but as we were completely accepted as Czech citizens in England, and as the teachers, administrators, and students did not discriminate against me in the Czech school in Wales, it did not occur to me that people who had been under brutal German domination for six years would not readily distinguish between Sudeten Germans expelled by the Nazis and those who had collaborated with them.

I had been too sheltered in England to be aware of the fact that the age-old enmity between Sudeten Germans and Czechs had risen to the surface with a vengeance throughout the war.

There now followed a long period of attempting to obtain the visa permitting my return to London. The British consulate insisted that I had been repatriated and that I now belonged to Czechoslovakia as a Czech citizen. I realized that my psychological feelings of "not belonging" would cut no ice with consular authorities and argued rather that, as a minor, my place was with my only living parent, my mother, residing in London and soon to become a British subject. For a year this wrangle continued.

Occasionally I also traveled in other parts of the country. Nostalgically, I visited my former hometown of Troppau, now known only by its Czech name: Opava. The town had been in the direct firing line of the advancing Russian army. Official reports claimed that 60 percent of the town was destroyed and lay in ruins when I saw it. Even so, much that I knew was still there, although true to form, everything seemed much smaller than I had remembered.

One afternoon during my stay, I visited my dear Tante Grete's sister, Alice, a dentist, whom as a child I had known only slightly. Looking pale and ravaged, Alice had recently returned from the concentration camp in Theresienstadt and was now reunited with her Aryan Czech husband. She was very ill with thrombosis and sat in a darkened room with her leg propped up on a cushion. Alice suddenly asked her husband to bring her a small wooden box. She opened it carefully and presented me with its contents. What I held in my trembling hand was my father's silver pocket watch, which he had given her for safekeeping. As my fingers closed around its curved rim, I finally realized the reality of my loss, and, for the first time since I had become aware of the disaster that had befallen me, I was overcome by tears.

# CHAPTER SEVEN

# Escaping the Nyilas

## *Hungary's Holocaust*

***Robert "Bob" Berger*** was born in Debrecen, Hungary, in 1929. When he was thirteen, he had to escape the ghetto to avoid being rounded up and taken to a concentration camp. His parents and two sisters escaped separately to Budapest. Bob participated in numerous Resistance activities, some of which are described in this account. After the war he ended up in displaced persons camps in Germany, but eventually got to America in 1947. Bob went on to have a pioneering career as a cardiac and pulmonary surgeon, including being deeply involved in the development of the artificial heart.

My psychiatrist husband, Irvin Yalom, met Bob in 1953, when they were both second-year medical students at Boston University. They struck up a close friendship, speaking weekly and often visiting, that lasted until Bob's death in 2016. Despite this intimacy, it took Bob half a century to talk to Irv openly about his experiences as a Jewish child in Nazi-occupied Hungary.

Irv's childhood experience of the Holocaust was closer to mine, but scarred him more deeply. For most of his life, he has found it unbearable to look at images of the Holocaust, or to contemplate the atrocities committed. Eventually, he found a way to approach it through literature, writing his novel *The Spinoza Problem* in 2012.

The conversations between Irv and Bob about Bob's experiences became the basis for a jointly authored novella: *I'm Calling The Police*. The following is an abbreviated print version of that Kindle book, and it is Irvin's voice that is the "I" in this narrative.

AS THE FAREWELL BANQUET of my fiftieth medical school reunion came to a close, Bob Berger, my old friend, my only remaining friend from medical school days, gestured to me that he needed to talk. Though we had taken different professional directions, he into heart surgery and I into the talking cure for broken hearts, we had established a close bond that we both knew would be life-long. When Bob took my arm to pull me aside, I knew something portentous was up. Bob rarely touched me. We shrinks notice things like that. He leaned to my ear and rasped, "Something heavy is going on . . . the past is erupting . . . my two lives, night and day, are joining. I need to talk."

I understood. Ever since his childhood spent during the Holocaust in Hungary, Bob had been living two lives: a daytime life as an affable, dedicated and indefatigable cardiac surgeon and a nighttime life when fragments of horrific memories tramped through his dreams. I knew all about his daytime life but in our fifty years of friendship he had revealed nothing of his nocturnal life. Nor had I ever heard an explicit request for help: Bob was self-contained, mysterious, enigmatic. This was a different Bob whispering in my ear. I nodded yes, yes. I was concerned.

But, was I ready to listen? Had I ever been ready to listen? It was only after I began my training in psychiatry and entered my own analysis and mastered some of the subtleties of interpersonal communication, that I grasped something essential about my relationship with Bob. It wasn't only that Bob was silent about his past: it was also that I did not want to know. He and I had colluded together in his long silence.

I remember as a teenager being transfixed, horrified, sickened by the postwar newsreels documenting the liberation of the camps. I wanted to look, I felt I should look. These were my people—I had to look. But whenever I did, I was shaken to the core and, even to this day, am unable to block the intrusion of those raw images—the barbed wire, the smoking ovens, the few surviving skeletal figures in striped rags. I was lucky: I could have been one of those skeletons had my parents not immigrated before the Nazis came to power. And, worst of all, were the images of bulldozers moving vast mountains of bodies. Some of those bodies belonged to my family: my father's sister was murdered in Poland, as were my Uncle Abe's wife and three children. He came to the U.S. in 1937, intending to bring over his family but ran out of time.

The images stirred up so much horror and generated such rageful fantasies that I could hardly bear them. When they entered my mind at night it was the end of sleep. And they were indelible: they never faded. Long before I met Bob, I resolved to add no more such images to the portfolio in my mind and began avoiding films and written descriptions of the Holocaust.

And so, after our classmates finally left the hotel banquet room amidst a chorus of "let's get together soon" and "so long for now"—with all of those white-haired wizened boys knowing down deep that they almost certainly would never meet again—we found a quiet corner of the hotel bar to talk. We ordered wine spritzers, and Bob began his tale.

"Last week I was in Caracas on a business trip."

"Caracas? Why? You crazy? With all that political upheaval?"

"That's the point. No one else in our group would go. It was thought to be too dangerous."

"And it's safe for you—a seventy-seven-year-old half-cripple with three stents in your heart?"

"You want to hear the story or you want to play therapist again with your one friend?"

He was right. Bob and I always bantered. It was a way-of-being unique to our relationship. I did it with none of my other friends. I'm certain our bantering was a sign of great affection; perhaps it's the

only way we found to be close to one another. The scars of his childhood and his many losses had resulted in his being unable to show
vulnerability or to express affection openly.

Unable to find either repose or safety, he had always worked at
a staggering pace, spending at least seventy to eighty hours a week
in the operating room or offering post-op care. Though he earned
handsomely from two or three open heart operations a day, money
was of little importance to him: he lived frugally and donated most
of his earnings to Israel or to Holocaust-related charities. In the spirit
of friendship, I could not stop nagging him about overwork. Once I
compared him to the ballerina in the red shoes who could not stop
dancing. He instantly responded that it was just the opposite: the ballerina was dancing herself to death but he was dancing to stay alive.

His remarkably fecund mind always generated new ideas and he was
renowned for developing a steady stream of new surgical procedures
that saved the lives of desperately ill people. When he retired from active surgery he fell into a long and profound depression but overcame
it in a remarkable manner. He became a scholar of the Holocaust and
entered the raging controversy about whether modern medicine should
use findings from Nazi medical research in concentration camps.
Ultimately Bob's epic paper in the *New England Journal of Medicine*
quelled the debate by proving that the Nazi research was largely fraudu-
lent. Action and effectiveness quickly ended his depression.

I knew he couldn't stop dancing. Nor could I stop proffering useless
advice to slow up, enjoy life, take time to call his friends.

But now, tonight at our fiftieth reunion, something had changed.
For the first time he asked me for help and I was resolved to deliver.

"Bob, tell me exactly what happened in Caracas."

"I was finishing a three-day trip. Because of the considerable risk of
robbery or kidnapping, my physician-hosts never left my side during
the entire trip. During my last dinner there, however, I told them they

did not need to accompany me to the airport: I had an early morning flight and the hotel would provide transportation. They insisted but I stuck to my guns and took the hotel limo. It seemed safe."

"Safe? Safe? With what's going on now in Venezuela?" I felt alarm about his judgment and started to protest but he wagged his finger at me and said, "There you go again—for nagging I don't need a shrink: I can get that anywhere."

"It's reflex, Bob, I can't help it. It's crazy-making to hear you exposing yourself to danger like that."

"Irv, do you remember after we had lunch in the deli yesterday and we were walking to the car?"

"Well, I remember our lunch. What does walking to the car have to do with this?"

"Remember we turned the corner and walked down the side street to the car."

"Right. Right. I chided you for walking right down the middle of the street and asked whether they had sidewalks in Budapest."

"There was more."

"More? What else. Oh yes, later I suggested that the street felt safer than the sidewalk because it afforded greater visibility."

"Well, I was too polite to say it then but you were totally wrong: it was just the opposite—I did it because it was more dangerous. That's the point—a point you've never understood about me. I was brought up on danger. It's programmed into me. A little danger soothes me. I've just realized recently that the operating room substituted for my dangerous life in the Resistance. In the operating room I lived with danger and faced it down with risky but life-saving heart operations. It has always been the place where I felt most comfortable. Mother's milk." Get it? the look on his face asked.

"I'm just a journeyman shrink working with the walking wounded and not accustomed to such extreme derangement," I said.

136

"Actually," Bob continued, brushing aside my comment, "for years I didn't appreciate I was different. I believed it was perfectly natural for anybody worth his salt to be in heart surgery and play the life and death game: those who were not interested in cardiac surgery or unable to enter the field missed out on the greatest challenge in life. It's only in recent years that I connected my passion for risk with my past. About twenty-five years ago, Boston University decided to set up an endowed chair in my name and issued a fancy glossy pamphlet. The cover had me in the operating room surrounded by all the assistants, surgical costumes and gadgetry, with the caption "To Save Lives That Could Not Be Saved." For decades I considered the caption just a Madison Avenue stunt to collect more money. Only recently have I realized that whoever coined that phrase knew me better than I did at the time."

"I've gotten you off-track. Let's go back to Caracas. What happened when you were picked up by the limo in the morning?"

"Aside from the driver overcharging me, the trip to the airport was uneventful. I asked to be taken to the main entrance of the airport but the driver told me that I would be closer to the check-in point if he let me off at a side door. As I entered the terminal, the airline counter was in sight only about 100 to 200 feet in front of me and I could see the passengers being processed through the gate. I had taken just a few steps when a young man dressed in khaki pants and a white short-sleeve shirt walked up to me and, in reasonably good English, asked to see my airline ticket. I asked him who he was and he told me he was a security policeman. I wanted proof and he flipped from his shirt pocket a plastic card written in Spanish with his picture on it. I handed him my ticket. He studied it carefully and then asked if I had enough cash to pay for the airport tax.

"'How much is it?'

"'Sixty thousand bolívars (about $20),' he said.

"I replied, 'That's OK.' When he wanted to see my wallet with the money, I assured him again that I had enough for the airport tax. Then he told me that my flight was delayed, and I should go with him up the stairs in front of us and wait in another lobby. He said he would help with my luggage and took my bag. Then he asked for my passport. My passport? An alarm rang in my head. My passport was my identity, my security, my ticket to freedom. Before I got my U.S. Citizenship and passport, I was a wandering stateless Jew. Without a passport, I could not go back home to Boston. I would again be a displaced person.

"Something was seriously wrong, I knew, and I went onto automatic pilot. Grasping my cell phone in my belt, I looked at him sharply and put my finger on the short antenna protruding from the upper right pole and said, 'This is a transmitter with a direct connection to the police. Give me my bag back or I'm going to push the button. I'm going to call the police.'

"He hesitated.

"'I'm calling the police,' I said. And then I repeated again louder, 'I'm calling the police.'

"He hesitated for a few seconds. I grabbed at my suitcase yanking it from his hand and started yelling—I don't remember what—and ran towards the security gate. Turning my head back for a second I saw my man running just as fast in the opposite direction. At the security gate, breathless, I told the agent what had just happened. He called the police immediately and, as he put down the phone, said, 'You are a very lucky man because you were about to be kidnapped. In the last month we've had six kidnappings at the airport and some of those kidnapped were never heard from again.'"

Bob took a deep breath, a long sip of spritzer, and turned to me, "That's the Venezuela part of the story."

"Quite a story!" I said. "And there are other parts?"

"It's just beginning. For a while I didn't truly register what had happened. I couldn't track: I was stunned, almost dizzy. But I didn't know why."

"Almost getting kidnapped is plenty—enough to stun anyone."

"No, as I said, that's just the beginning. Listen on. I went through security without trouble and was still in a fog as I walked to the flight gate and sat down. I opened a magazine but couldn't read a word. I waited about an hour, my mind swirling and then, like a sleepwalker, boarded the flight to Miami.

"During the three-hour layover in Miami I sat quietly in a comfortable chair, sipping a diet Coke. As I was dozing off, it happened: something that I had not thought about for almost sixty years forced its way back into memory. It was elusive at first but I yanked hard at it, trying to gather every detail. Eventually, an event in Budapest that took place sixty years ago when I was fifteen came sharply into focus. I was flooded with images and relived every detail. By the time I boarded the plane for Boston a few hours later, I felt relieved and almost free of anxiety."

"Tell me what you saw. Tell me all . . . don't leave anything out." I made my request as an act of love and friendship. I sensed that Bob would be relieved by sharing his experience but I dreaded what I was about to hear. But I also knew it was time to accompany my friend into his nightmare.

He finished the spritzer with a gulp and leaned back into the bar sofa. Closing his eyes, he spoke.

"I was fifteen. I had escaped from a column that the Nazis were leading from the Ghetto to the railway for deportation and I made my way back to Budapest where I was living as a Christian with false identification papers. Everyone in my family had already been arrested and deported. I was renting a room with a friend who had fled to Hungary from Czechoslovakia in 1942. He had lived for some time

139

with false identification papers and knew the ropes. Paul was his assumed name. I don't remember what last name he used and I never knew his real name. We became very close friends. Besides memories, I have an old wrinkled blown-up picture of him on the desk in my study. I had another close friend, Miklos, who was killed by the Nyilas a few months before."

"The Nyilas?"

"The Hungarian Nazis. They were barbarians, a militia of armed thugs who roamed the streets rounding up Jews and either killing them on the spot or taking them to their Party houses for torture and slaughter. They were more vicious to Jews than the Germans or the Hungarian Police. Nyilas comes from the Hungarian word for arrow. Their emblem was two crossed arrows, similar to the swastika.

"Paul and I were very close. When we heard about an uprising by Jews against the Nazis in Slovakia we wanted to join the Resistance there. Since I spoke no Slovak, he thought it best for him to go ahead to survey the situation. If things looked good he would find an underground channel and return to Budapest to fetch me. I went with him to the main railway station in Budapest and, as the train pulled out, I was certain that I'd see him in a couple of weeks. But I never heard from him again. I searched for news about Paul after the war, but could find no trace of him. I am sure that the Nazis killed him.

"I had a number of assignments from the Resistance, and did as much as possible when the occasion arose. Actually, I became pretty good at forging documents for Jews who wanted to pass as Christians. I earned my living from my day job as an all-purpose errand boy in a small factory that made medicines for the Hungarian Army.

"So here's the memory that returned last week at the Miami air terminal. I was fifteen, and one morning I was late and was rushing to work when I saw, across the street, a Nyilas thug—wearing an Army cap, a military belt, a pistol in a holster and the Nyilas armband with

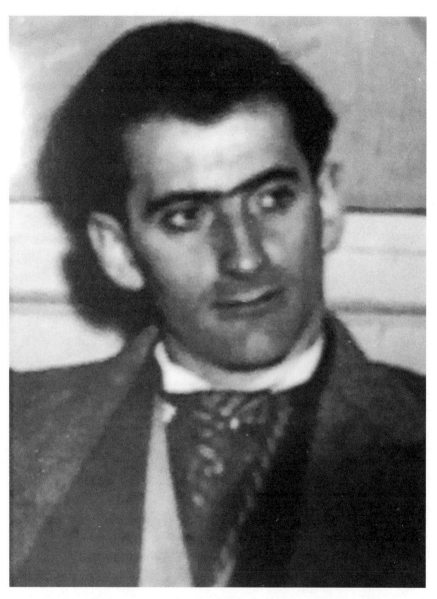

Robert "Bob" Berger, best man at a friend's wedding, Boston, circa 1950.

the two crossed black arrows—holding a submachine gun trained on an elderly hapless Jewish couple who were dragging themselves three or four feet in front of him. The Jews, probably in their sixties, wore the compulsory four-inch yellow star on their left chests. The old man had obviously been beaten, probably just minutes earlier: his face was so swollen and discolored you could barely see his eyes. His nose was also swollen, blue and red, twisted to the side and bleeding. Streaks of bright red blood were coursing from his grey hairline onto his forehead and trickling down his face. His ears were large, red and mangled. The woman cried as she walked alongside the man. I saw her turn her head backwards to plead with the thug but he just pushed her face back with the barrel of his gun.

"Keep in mind, this was nothing unusual in those days. I know it's hard to get your mind around it, but it was a standard scene all over the city many times every day. Jews were frequently apprehended on the street and sometimes shot on the spot. The bodies remained on the pavement for a day or two until they were picked up. Without doubt this couple was being taken to a Nyilas Party house where they would be questioned, tortured and shot in the head execution-style, or hung by a piano wire from a hook in the ceiling. Or shot and drowned both—that was one of their favorites. The Nyilas would march a group of Jews to the banks of Danube to shoot them and dump them into the icy river. Sometime three Jews were tied together and only one was shot but all thrown into the water. The other two died of drowning or froze to death."

I shivered involuntarily and had a premonition that the vision of the three bodies tied together, flailing in the icy river, would blast its way into my dreams later that night. But I said nothing.

Bob noticed the shiver and averted his eyes. "You get used to it, Irv; it's hard to believe but you get used to it. Even I can't believe now that it ever happened and yet, in reality, once it was an everyday occurrence. I saw several of these mass shootings and knew that, even if the shots were not fatal, the victims had no way of escaping death once they were thrown into the icy water.

"There were always Nyilas guards at the end and at the front of the columns of Jews led on the streets of Budapest. Sometimes, especially in the evening when it was dark, a Resistance fighter (I did this myself a few times) would follow them and throw a grenade at the guards, hoping to kill the Nyilas bastards. Of course the grenade would kill the Jews, too, but they were going to be dead soon anyway, and in the confusion occasionally some could escape. Such memories of my Resistance work never leave my mind. I know you are horrified as you hear this but I want to tell you that these were the peak experiences of my life.

"Another one of my assignments in the Zionist Resistance group was to follow Jews led on the streets by Nyilas thugs and to note the address of the Nyilas Party house, where they were taken. These houses were scattered all over the city, and if reports from various scouts like me indicated that a large number of Jews were detained in a given house, the place was attacked from time to time at night. Jewish youths in the Resistance on motorbikes would ride by the Party house, throw in hand grenades and rake the place with submachine gunfire.

"Although we usually targeted the upper floors of the building and the prisoners were in the cellar, we knew that some of the prisoners would be killed but we put that out of mind—the Jewish prisoners were doomed anyway. We just tried to kill Nazis. At the same time, we hoped that the confusion created by the attack would allow some of the Jewish prisoners to escape. In the larger scheme of things I'm sure our sporadic attacks were not very effective, but at least, we gave an account of ourselves, and the Nyilas knew they could not kill Jews totally unpunished; we wanted them to know they were in danger too.

"More details steadily drifted into mind. I remember that I did a doubletake when I saw the battered old man with his crying wife. Although I stopped and gawked for only an instant, probably not more than three or four seconds, the Nyilas guard noticed me and from across the street, turned his gun on me and bellowed, 'You—you get over here.'

"I crossed the street, trying to be casual. Facing tight spots and possible death was my daily staple and I kept my wits about me. I'm sure I was scared inside but couldn't afford to let fear take over: I had to concentrate on how to get out of the situation. You had to have a whole bunch of identification papers in those days to walk on the streets and although mine were false, they were well done and looked authentic. He asked me if I were Jewish. I said 'No,' and showed him one I.D. paper after another. He asked me where I lived and who I was living with. When I told him that I was living in a rooming house, his suspicion seemed to grow and he asked, 'How come?' I told him that I worked in a factory that made medicines for the Army in order to support a poor widowed mother and grandmother living in the country. And told him also that my father had been a Hungarian soldier who was killed on the Russian front fighting the communists. But none of this had any impact on the bastard. Only one curt response from him: 'You look like a Jew.' Then he pointed his gun at me and snarled, 'You line up with the other two Jews and get moving.'"

My anxiety was escalating. Bob saw me shaking my head and nodded his chin in a questioning manner.

"The horror of it, Bob. I'm with you. I'm listening to every word. But I can hardly bear it. My life has been so safe, so . . . so soft, so free of threat."

"You have to remember I lived with such encounters daily. As I walked next to the Jewish couple I knew I was in trouble enough, but there was something else; it suddenly dawned on me that something in my pocket could be really dangerous: three official Hungarian government rubber stamps. I had stolen them the day before from a store making these stamps and was planning that evening to meet my Resistance buddies to make phony documents for Jews to assume a Christian identity. It was dumb, really dumb, to be carrying such incriminating stuff on me for a whole day but I was determined to do the things that I had to do that night. All of us lived on the edge all the time.

"So that was the really big problem. I knew that I would be searched and when they found these stamps on me, I had no chance at all. Zero chance. They would accuse me of being a spy or in the Resistance. They would torture me for information about the Resistance—its location, the names of my buddies. After the torture, they would shoot or hang me. And I was afraid, too, that I would break and talk. I had to get rid of the stamps.

"Fortunately, I was carrying some genuine business letters, given to me to mail, from my factory addressed to Army headquarters. As we continued on our march I saw a mailbox across the street and realized that this was the big chance that I could not afford to miss. I yanked out the letters to the Hungarian Army from my bag, showed them to the Nyilas, and said that my boss told me that they had to be mailed today, as they contained dosage instructions for medication being shipped to the Russian front.

"I told the Nazi that I had to put those two letters in the mailbox across the street. He lowered his gun, examined the letters carefully, nodded okay but warned me not to try anything funny. While walking across the road over to the box, I slipped the rubber stamps from my pocket (thank God I only had the rubber part, not the wooden handle) and put them in-between the letters, opened the top of the mailbox and dropped the whole thing into the metal container. I felt a tremendous relief: I had gotten rid of a major piece of incriminating evidence. Now, I had only to get away by convincing the beast that I was not Jewish. There was always the possibility he might pull down my pants to see if I were circumcised. As I said, I knew I had zero chance if they saw the stamps but I also knew that if they got me into the Party house I had only less than five percent chance of surviving."

I couldn't be quiet. I was so anxious, my heart was pounding so hard, I had to say something, anything.

"Bob, I cannot imagine how you did this—how you got through it and have done what you've done in this life. What were you feeling inside? If I imagine myself in your position at the age of fifteen having to deal with almost certain death . . . I mean I can't imagine it. During my teenage years my greatest trauma was not having a date for New Year's Eve. It's pathetic. I don't know how you faced death like that . . . you know, I can deal with the thought of death now; I'm seventy-six, I've lived well, I fulfilled any promise I had. I'm prepared. But then at fifteen . . . the few times I remember thinking about death then . . . it was whooooosh—like a trapdoor opening beneath me . . . too awful to tolerate. I don't think there's any mystery about the source of your night terrors and dreams. I experience terror just hearing about your young life and I'll probably dream about your experience tonight."

Bob, patted me on the shoulder. Imagine, he had to comfort me. "You get used to things. Remember this was just one close call. One of many. I guess you can even get used to the overwhelming prospect of death. And remember, too, I was too preoccupied with survival to think of death. Just survival. If I let myself feel then—or even for the next twenty years—it would have been too much. You up to listening to the rest?"

I tried to conceal my quivering and nodded, "Of course." Now that Bob had finally privileged me with his secrets I was resolved never again to close him down.

"After walking another 10 to 15 minutes," he continued," I saw a Hungarian policeman turn the corner and walk towards us. I was desperate, and as soon as I saw him I must have said to myself, 'Here's my one chance, my only chance, to get away. I'm going to call the policeman.'

"I called out to him: 'Officer, officer, please sir I would like to talk to you. I was going to work and this man stopped me and won't let me go on my way. He is taking me somewhere. He claims I am Jewish but I am not. I hate Jews and I have papers to prove that I am Christian. If he does not let me go, I'll lose a whole day's pay, and I won't be able to send the money to my widowed mother and grandmother. Here, please, look at my documents. I'm Christian: these papers will show it and you'll let me go to work.' I held up and waved my identity papers.

"When the policeman asked what the problem was, the Nyilas thug snarled, 'He's a Jew. I'll take care of him and I'll take care of the other two Jews.'

"'Not here you won't,' barked the policeman. 'This street is on my watch. I'll handle this.'

"They argued briefly until the policeman lost patience, pulled his pistol and repeated, 'This is my area. I am patrolling it and I am taking this kid to the police station.'

"The Nyilas turned surprisingly timid and said that he would hand me over to the policeman's custody but would check with the police station to find out whether I was brought in. He then walked on, leading the old couple in front of him in the middle of the street. The policeman, still holding his pistol, told me to walk ahead of him. I turned and took a last look at that doomed Jewish couple. There was nothing I could do for them.

"There was a fair amount of antagonism between the Nyilas and the police because the police felt that the Nyilas were not professionals but a bunch of hoodlums who usurped legitimate police powers. Confrontations like the one I had provoked between the police and the Nyilas were not unusual."

Bob turned to address me directly—up till then he had told this story sometimes with eyes closed or looking off into the distance as if in a dream. His pupils were huge and, for once, I gazed right into them and after a few seconds prompted, "And then?"

"The policeman and I began to walk and after a block he put his gun back in his holster. He asked no questions and I kept silent. After walking a few more blocks he looked around and said, 'Scram and get to your job.' I thanked him and told him I was a Hungarian patriot and that my mother will be grateful to him. I kept on walking faster and faster and did not look back. Once I turned the corner and was out of the policeman's vision, I almost ran and when a passing streetcar slowed down I jumped on it. I was convinced somebody was following me. I spotted a policeman standing in the rear of the car and slowly edged my way forward to the front of the streetcar. After riding a couple of blocks, the streetcar slowed, and I jumped off and walked to work in a roundabout way, making certain that nobody was following me. When I walked into the factory where I worked the boss asked why I was late. He seemed satisfied by my explanation that the streets I ordinarily took were closed because of rubble produced by bombing the previous night.

"So, that's the story," Bob sat forward on the sofa and again looked straight at me. "What do you think? That's what you call repression, right? A half-century of forgetting?"

"No doubt about it." I said, "As clear an instance of repression—and of de-repression—as I've ever heard. We should write it up for a psychoanalytic journal."

"So maybe," Bob said, "your man Freud knew what he was talking about. Did you know Freud was one of us. He was almost Hungarian—his father came from Moravia and the whole region was all part of the Austro-Hungarian empire."

"What's particularly interesting to me is the tag that allowed you to pull it out of deep storage. The phrase, 'I'm going to call the police'—that was the link: it saved your life last week with the kidnapper in Venezuela and it saved your life when you were fifteen. Tell me, Bob, why did the Hungarian policeman let you go?"

"Yes, boychik, that's a good question. I was obsessed about that for a while but then life moved on. I asked myself many questions: Did he know I was a Jew? Was he a decent guy who wanted to do a decent act? Was he offering me my life in a spirit of generosity? Or was it he just did not feel like wasting his time on something as unimportant as me? Or did I matter at all—was I just incidental? Simply a lucky beneficiary of his hatred of the Nyilas? I'll never know."

"Any follow-up?" I asked. "What's happened in the week you've been back?"

"I hit the ground running and went directly to my office in Boston from the airport (there's no time zone difference between Boston and Caracas) and said nothing to my colleagues because near-kidnapping might scare away the group from setting up the clinical trial in Venezuela. In the next two weeks I go to half a dozen other cities."

"It's crazy, Bob. What are you doing? You're killing yourself. You're seventy-seven years old. I get exhausted listening to your schedule."

"I know that the new technique can make a difference to people who suffer terribly from emphysema, struggle for air and are slowly strangled to death. I enjoy doing what I'm doing. What could be more important?"

"Bob, the words are different but the music's the same. When you were operating you probably did more open heart surgery than any surgeon alive. Day and night—seven days a week. Everything in excess; nothing in moderation."

"So what kind of shrink friend are you? Why didn't you stop me?"

"I tried my best. I remember talking to you, nagging, yelling at you, cautioning you, exhorting you, until the day you gave me an answer that stopped me in my tracks. I've never forgotten it."

Bob looked up, "What did I say?"

"You've forgotten? Well, we talked about the reasons you lived so much of your life in the operating room. The major idea I put to you was that you had total control in the OR. It neutralized the sense of helplessness you had experienced when you watched your family and friends disappear. Though you had exhilarating moments in the Resistance, for the most part you were powerless—like millions of Jews. Above all you had to survive. Since then you've become insatiably active. You save lives. In the operating room you control almost everything.

"So that was my best guess," I continued. "But then one day you told me something else. I remember the time and place so clearly. We were at your home and you were sitting under that huge painting done in contra crayon of a mountain of gnarled naked bodies. That was where you always liked to sit. You seemed comfortable with that painting. I hated it and tightened up when I saw it and kept wanting to go into another room. And it was there that you told me that you felt truly alive only when you held a beating human heart in your hands. That totally silenced me. I had no answer."

"How come no answer? That's not like you."

"What could I say? You were saying to me, in effect, that to feel alive you needed to hang out in the wafer-thin membrane between life and death. I understood that you needed this danger, this urgency, to overcome the feeling of deadness within you. I felt then, as never before, overwhelmed by the horror of what you had experienced. I knew no recourse. I didn't know what to say. How could I fight deadness with words? I guess I tried to do it by actions. We had so many good times together, we did so many things—you and me and then our wives and our children and our trips together. But was it real for you? As real as the nighttime reality? Or was it evanescent, something penetrating only a millimeter or two? Bob, I know if I lived through what you've lived through, I'd either be dead or feel as though I were. Probably I, too, would want to hold a beating heart in my hands."

Bob looked moved. "I'm hearing you. Don't think I don't. I know you feel that I wrestle with my helplessness, the helplessness of all the Jews, gypsies, communists who faced the guns or marched to the gas chambers. You're right. I know I feel potent again when I perform, when I take control of the total environment in the operating room. And I know that I need the danger, the balancing act on the thin wire between life and death. I've taken it all in—all your words, all your actions.

"But," Bob continued, "there's another part, maybe an even bigger part, that you don't know about yet. A part you're about to hear. This part dwells only in my second life—my night life. It showed up in my dream."

I looked up in surprise, "What? You are going to tell me a dream? This will be a first."

"Consider it a fiftieth reunion present. If you get a good score interpreting it, I'll tell you another at our seventy-fifth reunion. My dreams . . . they almost always deal with one of two topics—the Holocaust or the operating room. One or the other and at times the two fuse into one. And somehow these dreams, horrible, brutal, bloody as they are, allow me to start the next day with a relatively clean slate. They serve as a kind of escape vent, they are like some maelstrom that parades and then bleaches dark memories.

"So, back to last week, to the day that started with the near-kidnapping in Caracas. I got home and told no one about what had happened. I was exhausted, too tired to eat, fell asleep before nine, and had a powerful dream. Maybe I dreamed it for you—a gift to my shrink friend. Here it is."

"It's the middle of the night. I'm in the waiting area of an emergency room that looks like the one at Boston City Hospital where I spent many nights over many years. I look at patients waiting to be taken care of. My attention is caught by an old man sitting on a bench with a bright yellow Star of David on his coat. I think I recognize him—but I'm not quite sure who he is.

"Then, I find myself in the locker room of the operating suite trying to change into scrubs. I cannot find scrub suits anywhere so I rush to the operating room in the striped pajamas I had been wearing under my suit. The stripes are blue and grey—yes, they are like concentration camp uniforms.

"The operating room is empty, eerie—no nurses, assistants or technicians, no anesthetists, no stands covered with blue drapes and loaded with surgical instruments neatly lined up and, most important of all for my trade, no heart and lung machine. I feel alone, lost, desperate. I look around. The walls of the operating room are covered with worn leather yellow suitcases stacked up in rows from corner to corner and piles from floor to ceiling. There are no windows—in fact, there is no empty wall space even for the X-ray view box—nothing but suitcases—suitcases like the one the old Jew was carrying in Budapest when he walked in front of the Nyilas thug pointing his machine gun.

"On the operating table, I see a naked man silently thrashing about. I walk over to him. He looks familiar. He is the same man I saw in the emergency room. And I know then, he is the doomed beaten man with the suitcase I saw on that Budapest street. He is now bleeding from two bullet holes through a yellow Star of David stitched to his naked chest. He needs immediate attention. I am all alone, nobody to help me and no surgical instruments. The man moans. He is dying and I have to open his chest to get to his heart and stop the bleeding. But I have no scalpel.

"Next I see the man's chest wide open, his heart, in the middle of the incision, is flabby and the beat feeble. With each beat the two bullet holes squirt jets of bright red blood upwards from the front wall of the heart into the air, splattering against the glass cover of the operating table lamp, producing a red blur on the bright light and then dripping back down on the man's bare chest. The holes in the heart must be closed but I have no Dacron surgical patches to close them.

"Then, suddenly, I have scissors in my right hand and I cut a circular patch from the bottom of my striped pajamas. I stitch the patch to cover one of the holes in the heart. The bleeding stops. The heart fills with blood and the beat becomes more vigorous. But then the second open hole begins to shoot geysers of blood. The heartbeat slows and the jets of blood grow sluggish and no longer reach the lamp but instead drip back on my hands as I work. I put one hand over the hole and cut a second circular striped patch from my pajamas. I sew it onto the edge of the second hole in the heart.

"The bleeding stops again but then, after a short time, the heart empties, the beat grows feeble and then stops altogether. I try to massage the heart but my hands do not move. By this time people begin streaming into the operating room, which now looks more like a court room. They all look at me accusingly.

"I woke up sweating. My sheets and pillow were soaking wet, and I kept on thinking as I woke: 'If only I could have massaged his heart, I could have saved his life.' Then I snapped awake, realized that the whole thing was a dream, and I felt less oppressed. But even awake I kept repeating silently to myself, 'If only I could have saved his life.'"

"If only you could have saved his life, then . . . then . . . Bob, keep going."

"But I couldn't save his life. No instruments. Not even a patch or a suture. I couldn't."

"Right, you couldn't save him. You were not equipped in the OR to save him. And you were not equipped as a fifteen-year-old terrified boy who barely saved himself that day. I think that's the key to the

153

dream. You could not have done differently. But still, every night you put yourself on trial and declare yourself guilty, and you've spent your life in expiation. I've been watching you for a long time, Robert Berger, and I have reached a verdict."

Bob looked up. I had caught his attention.

"I pronounce you innocent," I said.

For once Bob seemed speechless.

I stood up and pointed my forefinger at him and repeated, "I pronounce you innocent."

"I'm not so sure you've considered all the evidence, Judge. Isn't the dream saying I could've saved him by self-sacrifice. In the dream I cut up my clothes to save him. But sixty years ago on the streets of Budapest, I didn't think twice of the old man and his wife. Just tried to save myself."

"But, Bob, the dream answers your question. Explicitly. In the dream you gave everything you had, you even cut up your own clothes, and it still wasn't enough. His heart stopped anyway."

"I could have done something."

"Listen to the dream: its truth comes from your heart. You couldn't save him. Or save the others either. Not then and not now. You're innocent, Bob."

Bob nodded slowly, sat silently for a while, and then looked at his watch. "Eleven. Way past my bedtime. I'm going *schlufen*. What's your fee?"

"Astronomical. I'll need my calculator to figure it out."

"Whatever it is, I'll run it by the nighttime jury. Perhaps they'll award you a blessing or maybe a bagel and lox for breakfast." He turned, faced me directly and we hugged, longer than ever before. Then each of us slowly trudged off to our night of dreams.

# CHAPTER EIGHT

# When Memory Speaks

WHILE I WAS MIDWAY through writing this book, my friend Bram Dijkstra (the art and literary critic) remarked that I should question the veracity of childhood memories narrated thirty to seventy years after the end of World War II. Memory is fickle. It forgets most of the past, holds on to sketchy bits and pieces, blots out painful events, colors others in a more favorable light, and invents happenings to satisfy unconscious wishes. How, then, could a reliable book be based upon such unreliable accounts?

Without skipping a beat, he related to me an incident that had happened to him in wartime Holland when he was only two years old. Here is his version of the event, which I asked him to write:

> We were living in a part of the Hague at Het Mezen-plein 16, one of a group of middle-class houses in the bird quarter where all the streets were named after birds, *Mezen* meaning "titmouse." The houses encircled a *plein* (square) that consisted of a large, flat, very green, grassy area surrounded by a chest-high metal fence topped with several strands of barbed wire.
>
> It was a glorious day, sunny and warm, which is rare for Holland. My three sisters, ten, eight, and five years older than I were playing with a ball: bouncy, inflated, skittish. I must have been running after it along with them. Then one of them kicked the ball over the metal fence deep into the forbidden grassy territory, impossible

to retrieve. But my oldest sister knew what to do: big and strong, she picked me up and lowered me over the barbed-wire fence into the grassy territory, telling me to fetch the ball—which I did. Then all hell broke loose: there was first the very loud sound of airplanes and, almost immediately, ear-piercing noises, explosions all around, though not in the immediate vicinity of the grassy area.

Suddenly I saw my mother come running down the steps of our house, right in front of where I was standing, not knowing what to do. She screamed my name and signaled me to come to the fence, which I did among all the bursts of sound. She was very agitated and reached over the fence to pick me up, pulling me up so quickly that the barbs of the barbed wire tore through the clothes I was wearing, scratching my chest so much that my mother had to cover the scratches with cool plasters.

It is exactly this kind of event that a child would remember, not only because it was so intense at the time—literally written on the flesh and accompanied by ear-piercing explosions—but also because it continued to have symbolic value for the rest of his life.

Even so, Bram added a cautionary note about the unreliability of childhood memories:

One of the more intriguing questions about the reliability of personal memories and their effect on a child's psychological development is, ultimately, how much the details of such memories are influenced, contaminated, or altered by the concurrent experiences of those around the child when they occurred. In the case of my experience as a two-year-old, I know that it was real, indelible, and unforgettable. Seventy-eight years later, I can still feel the barbed wire scratching me, and I can still picture the scene, the colors, the event.

But everything I have written down has been buttressed by what other people—mostly my mother and my sisters—told me about it. I learned much later that this event took place a few days after the Germans invaded the Netherlands in June 1940. The whole area on the other side of the road adjacent to the *plein* where we lived was bombed to smithereens. Nothing was left standing. Damned, evil Germans destroying part of the city in which we lived. Fifty yards further and we might have been killed ourselves. I believed that event most of my life, thinking about the brutal inhumanity of the German invaders. Then, about fifteen years ago, my sisters and I revisited the grassy area—still surrounded by a barbed-wire fence, where it all had happened. At that time I learned that the planes that had bombed that area of our town had been British! It was one of the largest losses of civilian life in the Hague during the war. The British had destroyed that area and those who lived there in a futile attempt to create a defensive perimeter against the invaders.

In other words, what I experienced was real, and remained vivid in my memory. It unquestionably helped shaped my conception of reality: but the story surrounding it, which I built up over the years aided by reminiscences from my family and family friends, is only as accurate as those memories of others.

Here I disagree somewhat with Bram. Even if what he believed for many years has been contradicted by subsequent revelations, the event itself was real and significant in his life history. Even if the event has been altered, distorted, or exaggerated during the intervening years, does that make it less valid in terms of the injury done to the child's body and psyche? Does it make the initial experience any less traumatic? It turns out that the bombs had not been dropped by the Germans, but by the British. Does that alter the morality or lack of morality we have assigned to each side? What we "choose" to remember is more than the incident itself; it is also the accompanying affect. In this case, that affect is the fear that dwelled consciously and unconsciously with Bram Dijkstra for almost eighty years. He confided in me recently that the war was the source of a phobia which had kept him from flying by airplane until very late in life.

When I now read the stories of other European children—French and German, for example—who suffered bombardments by American and British planes, I cringe and ask if those bombings of civilian targets were truly necessary. We are still coming to terms with the firebombings of Hamburg and Dresden, not to mention the atomic explosions over Hiroshima and Nagasaki.

Gerhard Casper, the former president of Stanford University, remembered what happened in Hamburg in July 1943, when raids carried out by British and American air forces destroyed half the city of Hamburg and killed about fifty thousand people. As Casper wrote in his book *The Winds of Freedom* (Yale, 2014):

> My parents, my brother, and I watched that cloud from a distance. My father's survival techniques had included listening (illegally, of course) to German-language broadcasts from London. Because of British warnings of what Air Marshall Harris had dubbed "Operation Gomorrah," our parents took my brother and me to a village thirty miles east of Hamburg before the operation began. From there, we saw the intense orange glow of "Gomorrah" burning on the horizon.
>
> All I can remember from the war years are the air raids and a deep sense of fear and insecurity. We felt safe only when we knew that Hamburg was not a target. I shall not forget a starry summer night when we were all standing in the street while bombers were flying overhead: We were "safe" because their flight pattern and

height indicated that they were headed for Lübeck, the neighboring major city to the east.

Casper was seven when the war ended, and he remembers playing among the ruins of his destroyed city. He also remembers being fed after the war by American food supplies, which were delivered under the direction of Herbert Hoover, who had been U.S. President from 1929 to 1933, and who had a long history of overseas humanitarian aid dating back to World War I. Casper first heard the former president's name attached to the supplies popularly known as "Hoover foods," that were sent to German schools. The irony of history, as Casper wrote, is that forty years later he would literally walk in Hoover's footsteps: "Certainly neither I nor anybody else could have imagined in 1945 that one day I would become the president of Hoover's alma mater. Nor could anyone have imagined that my wife, Regina, and I would one day live in the Lou Henry Hoover House, the Hoovers' family home on the Stanford campus, which Herbert Hoover had given to the university in 1945, the year that World War II ended, to serve as the residence of the Stanford presidents."

Reading this account, I have tried to put myself in the place of those children terrified by the bombs dropped on them by my country. At the same time, my present revulsion regarding those events does not alter the fact that as a child I applauded the newsreels showing the destruction of German and Japanese cities.

In recalling incidents from long ago, it is often difficult to avoid an overlay of subsequently acquired knowledge. In the case of Philippe Martial, for example, he retained pristine memories of the washerwomen scrubbing away at the village washhouse, and of his grandfather's underground shelter where he and his sisters crowded together in terror during air raids, and of the triumphant arrival of the first American soldiers. These are all indelible memories that have the ring of unadorned truth. But elsewhere in his memoir, the adult man intervenes. For example, in Martial's observations of anti-Semitism and racism, the child was probably not aware of the Vichy government's decree that restricted the movement of Jews, Blacks, and other "brown-skinned people." It was enough for him and his sisters to have experienced racism personally when they were called "bamboulas" by the village children.

So, too, Susan Groag Bell would never forget the day she was called into her principal's office and told she had to leave the school because of her Jewish ancestry. In late adulthood she could still see the "large red-faced man" unable to meet her eyes and hear the "many lengthy pauses and clearings" of his throat, whereas most of her other childhood memories had been lost. As she explained at the beginning of her memoir, her difficulties in remembering her early life were undoubtedly related to the "unresolved shock" of having suddenly lost her stable home and "many of the people who created it." All that remained from the period before her eleventh year was "an unrecoverable haze of nostalgia." It was as if the event in her headmaster's office closed the door on a childhood of unadulterated happiness and ushered in a period of dislocation and sorrow.

Unlike Susan Bell, Winfried Weiss had an incredible memory that reached back to the age of two or three. In our lengthy conversations, I would question him over and over again about the accuracy of his memories. He would begin to relate an incident in such detail that I would have to stop him and ask: How old were you? How can you remember so much? Are you sure you are not just making this up? Finally he convinced me that it was all there in his head, and I convinced him that he had to write down his memories for what became *A Nazi Childhood*.

Yet, in shaping his written account, he also added documentation acquired as an adult. For example, he did extensive research to verify the attacks on his town, the types of British and American airplanes that had left such devastation, and numerous other facts unknown to a small boy. While this information gives historical credence to his account, it does not change his basic memories. What comes through most of all are the images, sounds, smells, loves, and fears of a child caught up in a world he accepted without question. Of course, he loved his father as well as his mother, and held onto the memory of paternal love long after he understood the atrocities his father had perpetrated as a Nazi. In Winfried's case, he tried to recreate his childhood as he had experienced it, without the judgmental stance of an adult who would have condemned his father outright. Instead, he does not disguise his childhood affection for his father nor his pride in Germany's military might, until 1943 when his father went off to die on the Russian front, and the tide turned against his homeland. His embrace of the Americans in the spring of 1945 demanded a rejection of his German past, which nonetheless remained within him, like some kind of snake-infested paradise. Winfried tenaciously held onto a reverence for his father, writing: "My father; my life's mystery. He became a model on which I was supposed to form myself. But his absence made it impossible. He became a metaphor. Whenever things went wrong, his memory was there to remind us of past times when his presence guaranteed the smooth order of things."

He held on, too, to an idyllic vision of his early childhood, in spite of the iniquities he recognized afterwards.

Stina Katchadourian had the advantage of her parents' carefully preserved correspondence dating from 1926 to 1945, that she did not read until many years later. She also spent time in archives in Stockholm, in Lapland, and in Helsinki, so as to underpin her memories with historical documentation. In addition, her sister, who was six years older, and an older cousin, also shared their memories with her.

It is clear from even the small sample in this book that individuals vary greatly in their capacity to remember. But whatever the number or exactitude of the memories that get imprinted in our minds, those included here had lifelong meaning for the individuals who recorded them. As for me, they have the ring of truth, with or without the accretions that were added afterwards.

In spite of so many differences in each story, there are also common themes they share. All of them, except one, focus on the wartime absence of the father. Philippe Martial lost his father three months before the war started and assumed the identity of an "orphan" that was to remain with him for the rest of his life. Winfried Weiss lost his father on the Russian front, and Susan Bell lost her father in a Nazi concentration camp. While we may feel that Winfried's father got what he deserved and that Susan's father was an innocent victim, both children continued to love and miss their fathers deeply for the rest of their lives.

Alain Briottet's father was a German prisoner of war for over five years during Alain's early childhood. Robert Berger was separated from his parents during his adolescence and was never truly reunited with them, although they both survived the camps, and ended up settling in Australia. Stina Katchadourian suffered the absence of her father while he was fighting against the Russians, but she had the good fortune of seeing him return after the war, and resuming life within an intact family.

Father absence during World War II did not affect only Europeans. Nearly one American family out of five contributed a family member to the armed forces, according to William M. Tuttle Jr. in his fine book *Daddy's Gone to War* (Oxford University Press, 1993). Tuttle recounted his own personal history of father absence in the preface to his book:

Born in 1937, I was a homefront child. My father went into the Army in late 1942 and returned three years later; we had all changed a lot in the interim. I remember many things about wartime: pulling my wagon around the block collecting bundles of old newspapers, playing war games in the lot next to our house in Detroit, and sitting with my mother in the kitchen listening to the war news on the radio. Both radio and the movies were important parts of my homefront world. . . .

I see that during the war my little brother George and I lived in a family of women headed by my mother, grandmother, and older sister Susan. Ours was a peaceful and, from my perspective, a happy one. But I wondered what our lives would be like when my father returned home, and I wondered what he would be like. . . .

I was seven when my father came home. Because I had not really known him before he left for the Army, I could not tell how the war had affected him. . . . We had missed important years together, and we never bridged the gap. My father died in 1962 at the age of fifty-seven. I believe that, in time, we would have become friends, but we never had a chance to do so. This has been the war's major legacy to me, and it is a sad one.

Tuttle was one of the lucky ones whose father came back, but, even so, the father's absence during the son's crucial early years left an emotional breach that was never fully repaired. There is no doubt that the absence or permanent loss of a father during wartime caused great psychological disruption and long-term anguish for children, whether they lived in the United States or Europe. Filling the void left by their husbands, mothers took full command of the household, sometimes with the aid of their own mothers or sisters. Many of them also became employed outside the home. Yet American working mothers were, as in my mother's case, frequently subject to criticism for "abandoning" their children. A public discourse arose around the so-called latchkey child, whose mother was deemed selfish for working in a factory or office, rather than staying at home to tend her offspring.

In Europe, almost all women, whether they worked outside the home or not, were thrust into roles previously held by men. Susan Bell's mother whisked her daughter away to England and worked as a domestic servant to support the two of them—a far cry from her prior role as the cosseted wife of a wealthy lawyer. Alain Briottet's mother negotiated the daunting move of her family from occupied Paris to the "free zone," where she took care of her children and simultaneously engaged in Resistance activities. Stina Katchadourian's mother shepherded her two daughters from Helsinki to far-away Lapland, and then, when Finnish Lapland became too dangerous, rowed them across the river to peaceful Sweden, where she found work in a refugee camp.

But sometimes, as in the case of Winfried Weiss, the mother's all-consuming presence was a mixed blessing. After his father's disappearance on the Russian front, Winfried lived in "a world of women" who "accomplished everything." His sense of identification with the women and longing for his father's presence would contribute to a lifelong hunger for strong masculine figures, even those, like Ray in his memoir, who inflicted pain.

At the beginning of the war, Philippe Martial relocated near his grandparents. It is not his mother but his grandfather who emerges as the hero of Philippe's wartime narrative. In the many conversations I have had with Philippe over the years, he has rarely had a good word to say about his mother, but his grandfather, his father, and his godfather, Gaston Monnerville, have remained in his memory as inspirational male figures. He tends to idealize the father he knew only during the first five years of his life—from all accounts, his father does seem to have been an admirable figure. Even so, this idealization of the lost father is shared by many other children orphaned at an early age. Subsequently, Philippe developed a form of reverence for Monnerville, his godfather, who became a surrogate father and mentor while he was growing up. And Monnerville, who had come from French Guiana with Philippe's father, was certainly deserving of reverence. As Philippe writes elsewhere: "As early as 1933, when he was already a deputy in the National Assembly, Monnerville gave a speech at the Trocadéro in which he denounced the German persecution of Jews. To continue the struggle and to defend his anti-Nazi convictions, Monnerville then entered into the Resistance. At that time, no one could have predicted that he would one day rise to the second-highest political position in France, as President of the French Senate from 1947 to 1968. Obviously, this has been a great source of pride for me and my sisters."

Only Robert Berger had little to say about his father. He was separated from his parents in his early teens, and somehow managed to survive on his own disguised as a Christian in wartime Hungary. Bob saw the worst of anti-Semitic horrors: Jews savagely beaten, shot, and drowned in a river, not only by Germans but also by Hungarian Nazis. As a teenager, he joined others in the Resistance and managed to retaliate by throwing hand grenades into Nazi enclaves. It is not surprising that he repressed many of his worst memories, some of which came back to haunt him later after an absence of fifty years.

Memory, then, has its own logic. We depend upon it to give meaning and direction to our lives. My own memories of World War II, conflated with my happy childhood, appear to me in the rosy context of family, friends, and patriotism. Only after the war, with the news of my mother's murdered relatives, did I begin to feel the unspeakable horror of the Holocaust.

My mother, Celia, was forty-one in 1945 when she received confirmation from the Red Cross that her sister, Regina, had died in a concentration camp. Celia was to live many more years, raise three children, successively marry and bury four husbands (!), and die peacefully at the age of nine-two. Several months before she died, she told me she had been receiving letters from Regina. Taken aback, I asked to see them. Impossible—they had been "mislaid." Why had she never heard from her sister before, I asked? Well, her sister had not been able to find her because my mother had had four husbands and changed her last name with each marriage. I gently reminded my mother that her sister had perished decades earlier. She refused to believe me. I did not press the point. For more than half her adult life, my mother had silently borne the memory of her sister's murder, and then, in order to die peacefully, she changed that memory into something she could bear.

I suspect that I have written this book, long after the end of World War II, because I have carried a lifelong sense of debt to the millions who suffered instead of me. And I despair as I see how many others continue to suffer. Even now, the lyrics from the Vietnam War era song circle in my head: "When will they ever learn? When will they ever learn?"

# Wartime Children as Adults

THE SIX MEMOIRS PRESENTED in this book bring us inside the experiences of children who survived World War II and lived into adulthood. Somehow they were able to incorporate their childhood memories into their grown-up personalities without becoming overly bitter or cynical. When I met them, they had all become decent, accomplished, honorable people. Let me reintroduce them in the order that I came to know them as adults.

Robert Berger came to the United States from a European displaced persons camp in 1947. In just one year of high school he learned enough English and showed enough promise to get himself admitted into Harvard University. From there he went on to the Boston University School of Medicine and to an outstanding career as a cardiac surgeon.

He became friends with my husband, Irv, when they were both medical students, and remained close until Bob's death in 2016. That friendship included me and Bob's wife, Pat, whom we saw regularly in Boston or at the Bergers' summer home on Cape Cod and sometimes at our home in Palo Alto.

His wartime experiences were central to his adult sense of identity. For one thing, his choice of a medical career and then of his specialty as a heart surgeon grew out of his desire to counter the evils he saw as an adolescent. As he once told me, when he had seen people destroyed so easily and so cruelly, being able to repair life gave his life its funda-mental meaning.

Bob was fortunate to marry a woman with as deep a moral purpose as his own. Pat Berger, also a physician, practiced internal medicine and at the same time was primarily responsible for raising their two daughters. Bob was driven as a physician, treating and operating upon an enormous number of patients. He worked excessively, did important research, published hundreds of scholarly papers, and was promoted to Professor of Surgery at the Boston University School of Medicine.

An important concession that Pat made concerned religion; she converted to Judaism. This was by no means an obvious choice, given that her grandfather, Harry Emerson Fosdick, was the renowned min-ister of the Riverside Church in upper Manhattan—a church with a long history of social activism. Bob proudly referred to his wife and her stalwart mother (still living today at 108!), as "Yankees," and with them he found a true home in America.

But Bob's horrific memories of World War II never left him. He fre-quently suffered nightmares and bouts of depression. We have seen in his joint writing with Irv how some of his most haunting experiences were repressed for more than half a century, only to return when he was confronted with a new, imminent danger during a foreign trip. He transcended his wartime memories by operating on hearts, vicariously reliving the life and death experience each time he held, massaged, or transplanted a living heart. In this way, he soothed survivor guilt and symbolically repaired the trauma he had seen as a boy.

Bob found an ingenious method for combatting one especially long period of depression that had lasted for several years. When he was no longer able to operate, he used his knowledge of medical method-ology to investigate some of the so-called research produced by Nazi doctors in the concentration camps, and was able to prove that the Nazi research was badly flawed and had produced false results. This

Bob Berger, Marilyn Yalom, and Irvin Yalom, on a tropical trip to Belize, circa 1990.

was more than a symbolic victory over his wartime enemies; it helped him regain the mental stability he needed to continue with his work as a physician.

When I first met Stina Katchadourian and her husband, Herant, in 1966, he had recently been appointed to the Stanford Department of Psychiatry, where my husband was already on the faculty. We developed a friendship that also included our children, Ben and Nina, which has lasted to this day.

It was clear to me from the beginning that Stina had lived a multicultural and multilingual life. Coming from the Swedish-speaking minority of Finland, she started off bilingual in Swedish and Finnish. In school, she studied German, English, and French and would later spend time in countries where those languages are spoken. She spent her junior year of college in the United States and, after graduation, spent almost two years doing social work in Peru, in the course of which she became fluent in Spanish. A later stay in Lebanon, where she met her Armenian husband, added Armenian to the list.

Stina has had a career as a journalist, as a literary translator, and as an author. She has published several English translations of works originally written in Swedish: poetry by Edith Södergran, Märta Tikkanen, and Tua Forsström and also prose works based on women's lives. In addition to her memoir of the war years, she also wrote a highly original book based on a document written in Armenian by her mother-in-law and translated into English by her son Herant (*Efronia: An Armenian Love Story*, 1993.) A play, a children's book in Swedish, and a multicultural cookbook soon joined the list.

All this I knew. But it was only after reading her wartime memoir, based on her own memories and on her parents' correspondence, that I began to understand how she had become the compassionate and empathic person that she is. As her memoir shows, she has known

Stina Katchadourian, circa 2013.

scarcity and hunger. She has learned through experience what it means to be a refugee. She has had friends who lost their fathers in the war. She has sat in bomb shelters and has been scared and cold. She has known what it feels like not to know what tomorrow will bring. She feels keenly the preciousness and fragility of life.

That is, I think, why in later life Stina involved herself in alleviating suffering through her journalism, through her social work in Peru, and through engagement in organizations such as Amnesty International and the Global Fund for Women. Her wartime experience left her with a deep sense of gratitude for having survived, and a readiness in her everyday life to offer help where she saw a need for it.

Stina has been a world traveler on a grand scale, accompanying and sometimes assisting her husband who has led educational trips around the world for Stanford University. But each summer, she returns to a small island off the coast of Finland where her family has had a summer home for four generations. In 2019, she and Herant celebrated their fifty-fifth wedding anniversary there. And with her two grandsons, she now picks blueberries for making pies in the same forest where her mother, during the war, used to pick them so the family would have something to eat.

Winfried Weiss came to the United States from Germany at the age of eighteen to live with his sister, who had married an American GI. He went to the University of North Carolina and then to graduate school in comparative literature at Harvard, from which we recruited him for California State College at Hayward where I was teaching in the mid-sixties. "From Harvard to Hayward," he once mused ironically.

From the minute we met, Winfried and I had what the Germans call *Wahlverwandtschaft*, an "elective affinity." With similar literary and cultural interests, we started a lively conversation that was to go on for the next twenty-five years. Not incidentally, I was drawn to his dark-haired good looks, that bore an odd resemblance to photos I had seen of Kafka. I was to learn that beneath that handsome exterior lay a truly Kafkaesque well of anguish, springing from his childhood during World War II.

In 1966, on his twenty-ninth birthday, I brought to work a birthday cake, which we finished off in his nearby garden. It was then that he told me something I had not anticipated. His father had been a Nazi. A police officer who had joined the national Socialist Party in the thirties. A bona fide, card-carrying Nazi.

I silently reproached myself: How could I, a Jew with relatives slaughtered in a German death camp, eat birthday cake with the son of a Nazi? Then, recovering my speech, I asked: "What happened to

Winfried Weiss with Marilyn Yalom, at the Yalom home, circa 1973, with Marilyn's sons Reid (standing) and Benjy (in front of Marilyn).

him?" The answer to that question would provide the starting point for his memoir published many years later.

As Professor of Foreign Languages and Literature Winfried was a popular teacher and well-liked among his colleagues. He published just enough scholarly articles to get promoted, but his real talent was in creative writing, as attested by his memoir *A Nazi Childhood* and other works, including *Stations*, published posthumously. The impetus for *Stations* was his long-time relationship with Robert Hagopian—a subject he was not ready to reveal to a general readership during his lifetime.

It had taken a long time for Winfried to tell me that he was more attracted to men than to women (which would, of course, have made him no more welcome in Nazi Germany than my Jewish relatives). Although he dated women and had had a few serious heterosexual relationships, he admitted that men were more important to him and that he couldn't imagine marrying because he knew he would not be able to give up sexual encounters with men. He recognized that his male fixation had taken shape in 1945 with the arrival of the American GIs and his strange encounter with Ray, though it had probably started even earlier.

Stepping back to 1973, when Winfried first met Robert Hagopian (Bob), as I wrote in the preface to *Stations* (Mosaic, 2000), I felt that Bob was the best thing that had ever happened to Winfried. After a series of mostly inappropriate lovers, Winfried had found his cultural and intellectual equal. Along with a PhD in music and an extraordinary talent as a pianist, Bob also had enormous personal appeal. In the 1970s, when gay men were coming out of the closet in the San Francisco Bay Area, Winfried and Bob became an "open" couple. Bob's Armenian family accepted Winfried without asking too many questions, and for almost a decade the two men enjoyed life together.

How could we have known then that a deadly disease would descend on an entire generation of gay men and leave few survivors? Even the medical profession didn't know what it was dealing with. What I remember most from that unspeakable year between the summer of 1983 when Bob was first hospitalized and the summer of 1984 when he died was Winfried's ceaseless devotion to him. I have rarely seen anyone—a spouse of either sex—take care of a dying partner with such constant love and attention.

Winfried continued teaching, traveling, and writing, but he lost much of his enthusiasm for life after Bob's death. When Winfried contracted AIDS in 1991, he went very quickly. We celebrated his fifty-fourth birthday on November 10, still hoping for a miraculous cure. Two weeks later he was dead.

After the war, Philippe Martial moved with his family to Paris, where he and his two sisters were placed in boarding schools. He had hoped to study mathematics in graduate school, but his poor health got in the way. For a time he was subject to mental breakdown and, simultaneously, he was hospitalized with tuberculosis. Philippe is the first to acknowledge that his wartime experiences marked him dramatically. Finally, he was able to study at l'Institut d'Études Politiques de Paris, a school for international studies designed to produce French political leaders. This led to his position in the administration of the French Senate, where his godfather, Gaston Monnerville, was already a considerable figure.

When I first met Philippe in the mid-1970s, he was head of the Senate's cultural services. During a career of over four decades, he ultimately became director of the Senate library, a prestigious position that held great responsibility and influence. Whenever a question was raised about the Senate itself—its history, building, grounds, and art collection—the standard answer would be: "Ask Martial."

Philippe not only published books on the Senate, but also poetry, including a collection of poems titled *Récital* which was honored by

Philippe Martial and Marilyn Yalom, visiting the home of the writer
Chateaubriand in Châteney-Malabry, circa 2010.

the Académie Française. Not surprisingly, one of the major themes of
his poetry is war. For his distinguished career, he has been decorated
by the French government as a Chevalier de la Légion d'Honneur, an
officer of the Ordre des Arts et des Lettres, and a Commandeur de
l'Ordre du Mérite.

We have seen in the selection from Susan Bell's autobiography how she
and her mother were obliged to leave Czechoslovakia for England in 1939
after Hitler annexed the Sudetenland. Susan's teen years in England were
generally pleasant ones, but after the war, she struggled to find her way. A
return to Czechoslovakia proved unsuccessful, and when she came back

to England, she contracted tuberculosis, which landed her in the hospital for almost a year. After a first, short-lived marriage, she met Ronald Bell, a British physicist, and they were married in 1959. Soon thereafter, he was offered a position in the United States, on the West Coast.

In 1964, while in her mid-thirties, she earned a bachelor's degree in history from Stanford University. When denied entrance to the Stanford history department's doctoral program because of her age, she pursued a master's degree at a smaller local university, Santa Clara, focusing on the subject of self-taught women of letters. In time, this led to a pioneering text in women's history titled *Women: From the Greeks to the French Revolution.*

I met Susan Bell in 1976, when I had taken a senior position at Stanford University's newly created Center for Research on Women (later renamed the Clayman Institute for Gender Research). With a record of publications in women's history, Bell was one of the first affiliated scholars we appointed at the center. She and I had many interests in common and formed a close friendship that was to last until her death in 2015.

In the 1980s and '90s, Susan and I taught several courses together, and we organized a conference that resulted in a book titled *Revealing Lives: Autobiography, Biography, and Gender.* Given her own eventful life, it seemed natural for Susan to end up writing her memoir. When she showed me her work-in-progress, I prodded her to overcome her British reserve so as to reveal more of her feelings. I had to persuade her to write something—anything—about her father's death. Ultimately, her highly restrained description of receiving her father's pocket watch expressed the depth of her loss. In the end, she produced a work that depicts her personal story within the historical context that shaped her life.

Susan did not have any children of her own, but she helped raise Ronald Bell's children, and became close to his son's family.

Susan Bell, from her book *Between Worlds*, 1990. Photo by Jerry Bauer.

Unfortunately, after some fifteen years, she and her husband struggled, with Ron wanting to live full time in England, and Susan in California. Eventually, they divorced.

It was about this time that a surprising event was to transform her life. She received a phone call from Peter Stansky, a professor in the Stanford University History Department, the very department that had refused her entry into its graduate program. He was calling to ask her to participate in a meeting of the Pacific Coast Conference on British Studies at Stanford. Not only was she thus recognized as a pioneer in Women's Studies, but she also formed a close relationship with Peter Stansky, that was to last to the end of her days.

They went to conferences in the field of British history together, and saw each other in both California and London, where she had kept her mother's apartment. They traveled as far as Czechoslovakia to see her hometown. Susan had finally found the perfect partner, and told me on many occasions that Peter was the love of her life. Until the very end, she had trouble believing in her happiness, after the tragedies of her early years.

I met Alain Briottet early in the twenty-first century, when I was half owner of a Parisian apartment, which I inhabited for several weeks every fall and spring. Alain was living just a half block away, and we quickly discovered many common interests, such as French theater. Our fledgling friendship reached out to include my friend Philippe Martial, forming a threesome that was ultimately responsible for the inception of this book.

Alain is now retired after a distinguished career in diplomacy, "undoubtedly chosen in reaction to the horror of war," as he stated in his 2016 memoir, *Sine Die: Gross-Born en Poméranie*. An earlier book, *Boston, Un Hiver Si Court* (2007), to appear in an English translation in 2020 under the title *Boston, My Wonderful Winter*, is a collection of short stories inspired by his time as the French Consul General in Boston from 1985 to 1990. Afterwards, he became successively the French Ambassador to Burma, Finland, and Bangladesh. From 2006 to 2012 he was the General Secretary of L'Association Georges Pompidou. For his service, he was made a Commandeur de la Légion d'Honneur in 2011.

When, fifty years after the end of the war, he was appointed ambassador to Finland and saw the Baltic Sea for the first time, his thoughts turned more and more to his father's imprisonment in Pomerania—the region in northern Germany and Poland which looks out upon the Baltic Sea. As he wrote: "The Baltic Sea had washed over my childhood. It was part of our family history. . . . From camps in Gross-Born to Arnswalde, my father never left the Baltic circle." Writing *Sine Die* was a way of paying homage to his father and to the other imprisoned officers whose memory had vanished from French history.

When I asked Alain recently what the longtime legacy of his father's absence during his childhood had been, he sent me the following account of an incident that occurred when he was on his way to Rangoon, where he was serving as the French Ambassador to Burma.

It was the beginning of September, 1992. I was at Roissy Airport retuning to Rangoon, and I called my parents. It was my father who picked up, though it was usually my mother who answered. His deep voice, which had impressed me when he returned from captivity in May, 1945, seemed to me even more weakened and fatigued over the phone. He said, "Your mother and I have been waiting for your call." I had the impression that it was he who was waiting for my call.

Alain Briottet when he was the Consul General
of France in Boston (1985–1990), 1989.

He continued, but his remarks seemed to come from another place and from someone else. "I hope that you haven't forgotten anything. Have you taken enough stamps for future letters? Your mother and I always wait for them impatiently. We read them right away to your sister."

After a short silence, he seemed to regain his breath and said, "Have good trip." And then in a strained voice, "Thank you for everything you have done for me."

My father died shortly thereafter on October 1, 1992.

For a long time I tried to understand what he meant in this final message. I've settled on an explanation, which today seems to me quite obvious.

My father was grateful that I always showed him the greatest respect. I always considered the man—yes, the man and not the father—as a courageous man, profoundly honest, hardworking, and kind. In childhood, I was well-behaved, later I was a timid and studious adolescent. During this period, I believe I never contested his decisions, differing from my brother and my sister, who had rebellious natures and needed to affirm their personalities. As a man, I consulted him on the decisions I made concerning my studies and my career. This respect was consistent with the emotional distance that had been established between us since his return. We did not want to alter or deepen it. And my father left me free to live my life. One day he said to me, "You are a serious fellow. I have confidence in you."

We had a tacit pact of mutual respect. I respected the captain.

What Alain Briottet doesn't discuss here are the psychological consequences of the return of a father after five years of captivity. His memoir, *Sine Die*, is very clear on that matter. In 1945, in a reconstituted household, the father had lost his privileged position; it was

Madame Briottet who assumed the multiple, demanding obligations of the marriage.

Moreover, hardened by unhappiness, separated from his family by the sufferings he had endured, Alain's father developed a protective shell which constrained the capacity for openness needed to talk to his son. Alain spoke personally to me and to Philippe of the difficulty both he and his father experienced in their conversations. On the whole, he had been raised by his mother during early childhood and had missed a paternal influence. As in the case of William M. Tuttle Jr., recounted in *Daddy's Gone to War*, the absence of a father marked him for life, and millions of others like him.

These six wartime children, whom I knew only as adults, had suffered horrors that I was spared on the other side of the Atlantic. We were more or less born in the same time frame—from 1926 to 1938—but for them, the war was the central fact of their early lives, and it continued to prey upon them into middle and old age. For me as a child, the war was something happening "over there," even though I cared about the fate of our soldiers and Allies and relatives living in England and Poland. After the war, when I first went to France, and then for the rest of my life, I think I sought out—consciously and unconsciously—people near my age who had experienced the war firsthand. I wanted to know how they had managed to survive, who had protected them, whether they had found comfort in religion and other institutions.

Most of my European-born friends living in America found an adult community within universities, which is where I met them; this is not surprising given my own life of university affiliations. Bob Berger remained at the Boston University School of Medicine and Winfried Weiss at Cal State Hayward (now Cal State East Bay). Stina Katchadourian and Susan Bell, while not faculty members themselves, were distinctly part of the Stanford community. Our universities offered an additional "home" for all of us, especially for Winfried who never married nor had a family of his own. My French friends found government institutions that provided permanent employment and a kind of ersatz family. To this day, long after retirement, I know that Philippe meets regularly with his former colleagues and that they even go on trips together.

As for religious support, this varied greatly among the six. Alain Briottet, for example, was grounded in the Catholic belief system of his mother, which has sustained him to this day, whereas Philippe Martial's doubts about Catholicism arose very early in life, and later he became an outspoken atheist. Winfried Weiss held onto the aesthetics and rituals of Catholicism—he often went to church for the music and sometimes lit candles for the deceased. Though he rejected the great bulk of church dogma, as an adult he regularly included a retreat among the monks at Assisi during his annual trip to Europe. After his death, as the executor of his will, I wrote to Father Salvatore at the Santuario di San Damiano in Assisi and received a reply saying that Salvatore would continue to pray for Winfried, "as he had earnestly desired."

Susan Bell, raised as a Protestant despite her Jewish heritage, had lost faith in all religions when I knew her, yet looked forward to celebrating Christmas each year with close Catholic friends. Robert Berger, who had suffered the most from being a Jew, held firmly to his Jewish identity until his death. Stina Katchadourian grew up in a Lutheran family which said evening prayers and celebrated Christmas. As a little girl, however, she skeptically wondered "why God created the Russians." Throughout her life, she has been nourished by religious art and music, and has not entirely ruled out the existence of a Higher Power.

Today, with half of these friends gone and my own life expectancy severely limited, I feel an urgency to publish these memoirs so that the lessons of World War II will not be forgotten. Children make the best witnesses. They are the innocent ones and cannot be implicated in the cruelty of their elders. Even today, with the world overwrought with violence, if we look to the children, they still give us hope.

# AFTERWORD

MY MOTHER, Marilyn Yalom, died in November 2019, while finishing this book. As we realized her days were very limited, she entrusted me to complete the edits of the manuscript. Reading through it, I was startled and moved by the stories it contains, and often delighted to learn more about the various writers, many of whom I have known since my own childhood. I also spent a great deal of time pondering what makes this particular collection stand out. There is no shortage of accounts of World War II, nor of the terrors of war for children. There are mountains of related scholarly research in numerous fields, from psychology to history and beyond. So why this book? Why this collection of people?

I can only give my thoughts through a personal viewpoint, connecting threads that run through these accounts to things I know about my mother, and filling in gaps with my knowledge of the writers when possible.

My mother was a scholar who delighted in spending long hours alone in library stacks or in her office at home, in communion with books and ideas. But she was not the introvert one might expect in such an erudite soul. On the contrary, she was very much a "people person," and had a large group of colleagues in whose work she was deeply interested. She always had plans to go walking with a friend, and she was never *not* in the middle of reading someone's manuscript or new publication. All the writers included here were connected in some way to this circle.

I grew up in this highly rarified world near the Stanford University campus, in which my parents' friends were brilliant intellectuals, fascinating writers, and accomplished doctors and scientists. This was due primarily to my mother's enthusiasm for interesting people with active, open minds. Many of these individuals have deeply specialized expertise, but all have something more as well: a curiosity about the world at large, and the capacity to see events through a broad lens, informed by multiple disciplines.

This trait is unmistakable in the wonderful group of stories in this book. The protagonists are all people who have, or had, a broad perspective on the world. The narratives are both personal and worldly and the overall effect is rich, multifaceted, and powerfully humane.

That my mother was instrumental in bringing these people together is no surprise. One of her skills was the ability to help people articulate their own ideas. She was interested in people, their experiences and reflections, and was a master at coaxing out information, almost unnoticed.

What most marks all of her books, I think, was her ability to connect specific events or thoughts to larger ideas in history or literature. With *The Amorous Heart* or *Birth of the Chess Queen*, for instance, she was able to take a single, simple, idea and use it as the jumping off point for a great discussion of ideas and history. A personal example: I have worked with foolsFURY, a small experimental theater ensemble in San Francisco, for the last twenty years. One night we asked my parents to lead a post-show discussion following a performance of *The Unheard of World* by French playwright Fabrice Melquiot. It is an odd and delightful play, set in a fantastical city among the roots of trees where the spirit of every person who has ever lived resides. This city also contains the Museum of Plaster Casts, where the mold for every first object in the world is kept—the first bicycle, the first book, the first hand that killed. These are critical to the plot, and in rehearsal they were a fun quirky concept to play around with.

In the post-show discussion, however, my mother quickly took it further, connecting to the idea of Platonic forms, and relating the underground world itself to the cave in Plato's parable. She went on for ten or fifteen minutes, grounding this seemingly light and whimsical play deep in the soil of Western philosophy and literature.

Later, a couple of the actors told me they had been surprised and impressed by this analysis, and hadn't thought of any these ideas as we worked on the play. I shrugged it off. This broad intellectual playfulness was standard fare at my mother's dinner table. Wasn't it at everyone's? (I now have three small children, whom I can't convince to sit at the dinner table for more than ninety seconds before they begin to throw food, run laps around the room, and insist on watching TV. So my grasp of reality has improved.)

This tendency to connect ideas and see bigger pictures was not just hers, of course. It is present in all of the narratives in this volume. Each of these writers offers us their account of childhood during wartime, replete with specific objects and events—a rubber stamp or an imaginary friend, huddling in a damp cellar during a nighttime raid, or being dismissed from elementary school for an unnamed sin. But the telling is through adult eyes, colored with awareness and introspection, offering a kaleidoscopic vision of childhood during trauma, told by a group of profoundly insightful people.

This ability to blend perspectives, to simultaneously encompass the direct youthful voice and the more reflective adult one, is a trait of great writing. And this book is also a testament to my mother's love for literature, to the walls of the home she and my father made together, thick with books from floor to ceiling, and weekends spent reading the *Times Literary Supplement* and the *New York Review of Books*.

My mother met my father, Irvin Yalom, when they were both in middle school. They were married for sixty-seven years. Reflecting on what made their marriage so enduring, my mother always credited my father's "great capacity to love." And while she generally gave him the credit, she too, uncontestably, had this characteristic in great supply.

Love and empathy are deeply intertwined, and all the writers in this collection are deeply empathetic souls, full of warmth and love. We, fortunate readers, get a series of deeply insightful accounts infused with observations, wisdom, and a deep, compassionate, humanity. So, open minds and open hearts. Ultimately, I think it is this combination that makes this collection stand out.

There is another important element to this collection which I suspect was not conscious on my mother's part. Here we have a remarkable group of people who have done impactful things with their lives, becoming surgeons, educators, diplomats, writers. Rather than being broken by their traumatic experience of war (as many are), it seems these experiences may have, instead, nurtured in them personal characteristics such as the desire to make lasting and positive contributions, a type of empowering ambition, and a deep warmth and kindness. Bob Berger was compelled by his war experience to become a heart surgeon, to save as many people he could in the most direct and raw way possible; Alain Briottet became an ambassador for the French government, working to avoid conflict on an international level; Stina Katchadourian has spent decades nurturing cross-cultural understanding through her writings and translations.

Who is to say what these people would have become without their wartime experiences? I can only suggest that these accounts of youth hold the roots of what many of them came to be, and the pressures of war may have served as catalyst for some of their best qualities. We often think of the soldiers who sacrificed to defeat the Axis powers, referring to them as the "Greatest Generation." But what of those who were deprived of the innocence of childhood by the war, who grew up amidst these terrors, and yet managed to hold onto hope, and to manifest great things in the world?

In her last years, my mother despaired greatly about the state of the world, and the populist turn our country has taken. She saw current politics in the United States as a bitter reversal in the progress of rights for women, for which she had been fighting for many decades, as well as a reversal in the rights of minorities, and a meanness and negative spirit that she sensed soaking into the fabric of this country which she loved. I was visiting in the midst of the Brett Kavanaugh hearings, and came to breakfast one morning to find her drinking her morning tea, deeply upset. She had had a nightmare, she explained, in which a group of old white men were screaming at her. No subtle dream interpretation needed here!

It remains to be seen what will come of this era. While we in America will likely not suffer a "hot" war on our own territory, our children will be deeply impacted by their experiences of this period. Watching my own children as they struggle to make sense of the world, I try to explain in useful terms the things they see: regular killings of Black people by the very police officers who are supposed to protect and serve them, crowds of angry people screaming that doctors are murderers, or the fact that thirty-five miles from here, on the Mexican border, we are literally ripping thousands of children from their families with no promise of reunion. Perhaps the one hopeful thought I could have offered my mother is that these terrible experiences will also nurture fine shining souls, like those she chose to make her friends.

My mother worked with many of the writers here, drawing out stories, editing manuscripts, and offering encouragement. Working on this manuscript has been a wonderful, and emotionally fraught, act of communion with her. I am deeply grateful to have had this final collaboration.

BEN YALOM
June 2020

# ACKNOWLEDGMENTS

IT WAS IN PARIS in October 2018 that Alain Briottet, Philippe Martial, and I came up with the idea for this book. Each of us would contribute a section, and we would garner others from friends who were also children during World War II. After I returned to the United States, Alain and Philippe accompanied me by email at every stage of writing and editing.

Stina Katchadourian, who contributed a section of her memoir, also read the manuscript and suggested important changes.

When the manuscript was almost complete, historian Mary Felstiner critiqued the work in detail. It was her idea to add a final chapter on the wartime children as adults. I am grateful for her steadfast support as I worked to make this book as significant and as readable as possible.

As always, my literary agent, Sandra Dykstra, was a source of great encouragement.

Most important, my husband, Irvin Yalom, provided the emotional support and literary context we have shared in our long life together.

### EDITOR'S NOTE

As I describe in the afterword, my mother, Marilyn Yalom, left the completion of this book to me when she passed away. Fulfilling her request reintroduced me to many of the writers and friends whose stories are presented here. Some of them I was able to call when questions arose. In other cases, I have had to access both the source material, and memories from my own childhood. My profound thanks to Stina Katchadourian, Philippe Martial, Pat Berger, and Mary Felstiner, who have helped me through the editing, and my wife, Anisa Yalom, who has helped me with everything else.

# CREDITS

Chapter 2 is translated from *Sine Die: Gross-Born en Poméranie* by Alain Briottet. © Éditions Illador, Alain Briottet "Sine die", 2016. Reprinted with the permission of Éditions Illador.

Chapter 3 is published with the permission of Philippe Martial.

Chapter 4 is excerpted from *A Nazi Childhood* by Winfried Weiss. © Winfried Weiss 1983. Reprinted with the permission of Mosaic Press.

Chapter 5 is excerpted from *The Lapp King's Daughter: A Family's Journey Through Finland's Wars* by Stina Katchadourian. © Stina Katchadourian 2010. Reprinted with the permission of Fithian Press, a division of Daniel & Daniel, Publishers.

Chapter 6 is excerpted from *Between Worlds: In Czechoslovakia, England, and America* by Susan Groag Bell. © Susan Groag Bell 1991. Reprinted with the permission of Laura Mayhall.

Chapter 7 is excerpted from *I'm Calling the Police* by Irvin D. Yalom, copyright © 2011. Reprinted by permission of Basic Books, an imprint of Hachette Book Group, Inc.

Chapter 8 includes excerpts from *Daddy's Gone to War: The Second World War in the Lives of America's Children* by William M. Tuttle, Jr. © William M. Tuttle, Jr. 1993. Reprinted with the permission of Oxford University Press. Portions of Chapter 8 are published with the permission of Bram Dijkstra.